Anne Alcock

Texts and .... ɔr
Spiritual Directors

INDIVIDUAL GUIDANCE, PERSONAL PRAYER
OR GROUP WORK

the columba press

First published in 2006 by
the columba press
55A Spruce Avenue, Stillorgan Industrial Park,
Blackrock, Co Dublin

Cover by Bill Bolger
Cover photo by Carol Dorgan
Origination by The Columba Press
Printed in Ireland by ColourBooks Ltd, Dublin

ISBN 1 85607 550 8

Acknowledgements
I say thank you for those who first showed me the breadth and the depth which is possible in the ministry of spiritual direction, namely Gerard W. Hughes SJ, and Peter Van Breeman SJ.

More recently, for a supply of questions, suggestions, critique, proof-reading, advice, or support, I say thank-you to Elizabeth Bradley OSU, John Bennett MSC of Grace Dieu Spiritual Accompaniment Programme, Carmel Boyle of An Croí Spiritual Guidance Holistic Training programme, Michael Collender OSA, Mary Dinneen PVBM, Carol Dorgan, Louis Hughes OP, Jo McCarthy RSM, Gerard Norton OP, Helen O'Callaghan-Hoffman, Geraldine Holton of An Croí Spiritual Guidance Holistic Training Programme, Geraldine O'Mahony OP, Joan Sreenan MIACP, Liam G Walsh OP and all the directees I have been privileged to accompany over the last thirty years.

Scripture quotations are taken from the New Revised Standard Version, copyright © 1989, by the Division of Christian Education of the National Council of the Churches of Christ in the United States of America. Used by permission.

Table of Contents

Dedicated to Bonaventure Perquin OP and Frank J. Houdek SJ

Introduction

Tips are succinct. Tips do not stand alone. They do not involve over-explanation, since they are implicitly connected to a wider base of expertise or familiarity which provides their frame of reference.

Tips are sharable, in an 'over the garden fence' kind of way. The tips here are offered out of thirty years' experience, but do not presume in any way to be a final word, nor of course, are they totally comprehensive. What is presented are short answers to genuine questions which I have been asked over the years, have asked myself, and still hear people asking, both directors and directees. Whatever the answers, the questions seem valid at whatever stage we may be in this ministry. Many questions will be addressed in books and courses, but a few seemingly obvious but still important ones may fall between the two, and if so, I hope these brief reflections on practice will offer a further perspective from which to proceed.

As such, although they may be particularly relevant to the newer spiritual director, some may offer further reflection to those who have spent longer in this ministry – a kind of fine-focusing,

As to the compilation of texts, my favourite occupation as a child was taking all the books out of my smallish bookcase, to spend some happy hours 'sorting them'. Whether by category or author, colour or size, provided they were organised for practical use, I was happy. (Then I would start on my brother's bookcases!) When I later learned that the word Bible loosely means 'library'[1] I was even happier, and have been involved in some way with 'sorting' that scriptural collection ever since. This selection of scripture texts is broadly categorised under specific themes from a psycho-spiritual perspective. I say broadly, because these, and especially the annotations alongside, are sug-

1. *biblia* – conveying the sense of a multiple of books.

gestions, not definitions. I trust, however, that the themes and sub-sections identify some of the psychological and spiritual involvement we can have with the living word of scripture, and as such will be useful in one-to-one sessions, retreats or prayer-group work. You will notice that the texts are fairly similar in length, and show only the most 'well-known' verses. This is deliberate and based on the belief that we are probably sufficiently familiar with the content of most scripture passages to recognise 'this is the one' after the first few lines. You will notice 'ff' after many of the more truncated gospel stories – this indicates that the whole text can then be sourced as appropriate. For easy reference, the main category headings are in themed alphabetical order. A chronological list of the texts is given as is an alphabetical list by scriptural subject. All the texts are taken from the NRSV, except for one or two as indicated.

Alongside the texts and tips, I have included a few kernels of wisdom from the experience of some of the current well-known spiritual directors, that will hopefully offer an inspiring and energising echo to those of us engaged in the ministry of accompaniment, guidance, or as it is best known, 'spiritual direction'. A term which perhaps does not best describe the role, (since we know that spiritual direction concerns more than 'the spiritual' and we know that we are less a 'director' than an 'enabler'), but as a working term, spiritual director does have accuracy if used to describe a life process. Spiritual Direction, as Sandra Schneiders puts it, is 'a process ... of establishing and maintaining a growth-orientation (that is, direction) in one's faith life.'[2]

---

2. Schneiders, Sandra, *Selling All, Commitment, Celibacy and Community in Catholic Religious Life* (Mahwah NJ: Paulist Press, 2001), p 45.

Index of Tips

Tips

> 'There is something unique about this type of relationship that requires a deep level of commitment of the spiritual director to the process of enabling the encounter between God and the directee to come alive in the session. There has to be a depth of commitment to the directee and a fundamental belief that God desires to reveal Godself to everyone. It is through grace that directors are able to achieve this balance. The ministry of spiritual direction is a charism.'[2]

THE QUESTIONS

What do I need to 'become' a spiritual director?

A phrase that comes to mind is 'a sense of call,' which implies something rather different from simply a 'career option'. There may be a background in spirituality, theology, or counselling, and one essential is the experience of being in spiritual direction, and of course maintaining an on-going personal relationship with God .

Does the word 'holistic' fit in with being a spiritual director, or is it mostly scripture?

The word 'holistic' is what we now understand as lived experience – body, mind and spirit. Ways of being responsive to, and attentive to the God-in-all things, others and oneself is what the spiritual life is about. We will experience God's presence in many ways, through nature, movement, dance, poetry, art, companionship, intimacy; in the sacred writings of our tradition, and in liturgies and ritual. Increasingly many Christians are also reading the wisdom-words of other religious traditions. In this book, the emphasis is on texts from the Judaeo-Christian tradition, Old and New Testaments, as a template against which we

---

2. Margaret A. L. Blackie, 'Finding the Hot Slots; An Ignatian Contrast to Parent and Friend Models of Spiritual Direction.' *Presence – An International Journal of Spiritual Direction*, Vol 12 No 1 Mar 2006.

can find our own life experience, and pray and act out of that. And to be authentic, that living out will always be holistic.[3]

How do I make sure I have 'good boundaries' in the one-to-one-ness of spiritual direction?
The answer here perhaps best comes from asking yourself questions such as: From where do I draw my primary sustenance – body, soul and Spirit? Do I claim a sustaining life for myself, alongside my work, or is it from my directees that I meet my emotional needs?

How easily can I let directees move on and away?
Do you find yourself reluctant to let them go? Do you find yourself carrying them around, feeling anxious, tired and 'burdened'? Are you are doing the directees' work for them? Over-engaging mentally or emotionally? Yes, we need to be engaged with the story and process of the person to whom we are listening, but this always requires a measure of objectivity and detachment, because, as Ursula O'Farrell points out, 'if we become too emotionally involved, our perspective narrows to theirs.'[4] Concomitant with this, how 'curious' are you? Do you find yourself wanting to hear more of a story in a 'gossipy' way, rather than being content to stay with the overall meaning for the other person, even if you never get to hear all the extra details? You might even dare to ask yourself, Do I take my clients to bed with me? That is, keeping them with you in dream or in fantasy. Not healthy for them, not healthy for you.

What about physical contact, like when someone asks for a hug?
It is likely that you will occasionally be asked for a hug. For reassurance, perhaps, in a specifically critical moment. Of course the usual ethical boundaries for professionals obtain here, and in

---

3. The original 1st and 2nd century teaching of the Christian church clearly affirmed the unity of body-soul and remains true to this, even though this did often get distorted in actual practice.
4. O' Farrell Ursula, *First Steps in Counselling*, (Veritas, Dublin) 1988, p 33.

the counselling world this is normally a no-no, so it is up to the spiritual director to decide in the light of these, and the role, whether she/he responds to the request. Key words might be *occasionally* and *specifically*, never *always* and *everywhere*.

> ... we must be particularly reverent and respectful of the sacred trust of our directees and constantly help them shift their primary focus away from their relationship with us and toward their primary relationship with God. [5]

Suppose it is the director who simply wants to 'give a hug'– No big deal?

Whose needs are being met here? How does the director know there are not difficult sexual issues in a person's past life which might never have been mentioned in spiritual direction?[6] A directee's boundaries, physical and psychological, cannot be tampered with, however benign the intention. I believe it is never appropriate for the director to initiate hugging. This is a role relationship, which therefore carries within it an implicit power which may not be used to activate even the possibility for feelings of distress, un-freedom, false compliance, confusion, or long-term dependency, either way.

That may be all right for comings and goings, but what if someone is crying?

How comfortable are you yourself with tears? What do tears mean for you? Ultimately, crying is cathartic, and stress-relieving. In fact tears-of-sadness have been found to contain a particular constituent which is calm-inducing, not found in joyful tears. So how do we allow someone to 'weep well'? At some time or other, we have all said, 'It's all right, don't cry' to our friends and relatives. However in this relationship, once we our-

---

5. Ruffing, Janet K, RSM, *Spiritual Direction –Beyond the beginnings* (Mahwah NJ: Paulist Press, 2000), p 172.
6. Working with disclosure of this kind may of course more properly belong to psychotherapy, or at least presuppose further appropriate training on the part of the director.

selves are comfortable around tears, it is better to say 'Do cry, That's all right' and allow someone the space to do just that, without intruding even our 'helping self' into that moment of private grief. This may be a meeting, an ending, a recognition, a naming – it is their privilege, to be there in God's presence and in your presence. In that order. Yes, the person knows you are there, has relaxed enough to be able to cry, and you remain completely 'with them,' holding the space, holding the silence, respectful, empathetic – I may slip a tissue into a hand, unobtrusively, and eventually (not at the first tear as a worried signal to 'dry up now') and I wait, not rushing in, and I pray, and yes, specifically, and on this occasion, when grief is spent, and it is time to go, sometimes a pressure in the handshake, the taking of two hands, or a press on the shoulder will re-affirm that you are there, alongside, lovingly.

> Spiritual direction is a kind of discernment about discernment.[7]

Suppose I find myself concerned about something that came up in the session, and continue uneasy afterwards?
This is one of several reasons why it is important to try and have some space between appointments. As you take some time to try and locate the source of this, you might be distinguishing, What triggered this in particular? When? Who is this about? The directee? Me? Is there something I need to address or bring up next meeting? Is this something I need to take to supervision?

When you have reflected and discerned, and decided the next course of action as far as you can do so for now, the time comes when you surrender the person lovingly back to her/his life in God, and then move on peacefully with yours. It may be useful to bear in mind the reminder I once heard: 'The Lord is with you, and the Lord is also with them. Go in peace.'

---

7. Bakke, Jeanette A, *Holy Invitations – Exploring Spiritual Direction*, (Grand Rapids MI: Baker Book House Company) 2000, p 18.

Someone talks about suicidal feelings. What do I do?
Is this catharsis from the past, or a present possibility? If the latter, then the point you will have made at initial interview about confidentiality not guaranteed where harm to self or others is at stake, will apply. When feeling outside one's own area of professional competence, refer.

Whom do I call if I feel someone is a) seriously disturbed, b) potentially suicidal?
The doctor is the one enabled to enact the mental health act in these circumstances, and alongside the usual customary details for a professional relationship, (name etc) it is useful to list the name and number of a person's GP.

We talk about a person's 'spiritual life', but what marks out a spiritual life from any other?
Spiritual life is perhaps the attitude with which 'ordinary' life is lived, the 'God' filter through which we see and act, and what we are doing to deepen and nourish that – and spiritual direction is one of the ways.

Often in spiritual direction, those who are not used to being listened to will tell marvellously rich life stories, only to end with an apology for taking up time ...

For the directee, simply to tell one's story and to be listened to is a healing and liberating practice ... The role of the director as witness is to listen and to look, not just at reported facts but also at how the person understands what happens in his or her life. This does not mean that the director ignores his or her own perceptions. But it does mean that the director stays with the unfolding story, not stopping, not offering premature closure or resolution. This takes patience and faith in the story one is witnessing come to life. (Juan Reed, *Can I get a witness? Spiritual Direction with the Marginalized.*)[8]

What makes a person a good spiritual director?
Is this a bit like the parable of the fig tree? A good tree and its fruits? A wise director and God's fruits? What would you expect

from your own spiritual director to qualify as 'good'? Assuming adequate training and skills, unconditional positive regard and confidentiality, we could be talking about someone, lay, cleric, married or single, for whom a spiritual life is their own Way of Life. However, added to this also someone with sufficient experience behind them to have worked positively through the 'stretchings' of some significant life-events, and has a sense of life's terrain.

Someone who honours the time for the ministry of spiritual direction as a priority, rather than just 'fitting someone in' between other work. And finally someone who, because ego is stepping aside for the deeper self, humbly acknowledges that she/he will always be sitting there as assistant, receiving guidance.

What is the difference or overlap between spiritual direction, counselling or life-coaching?
A question every book will be answering, both longer and better, but as someone involved in all three, I offer these distinctions, focusing simply on perceived intention. Spiritual direction intends to facilitate and nourish the relationship between God and the individual. God is the agreed focus and thus the process is three-way. Counselling (widely generalising, here) intends to assist in easing or teasing-out what prevents someone from 'living' with inner freedom, and uses a specific psychotherapeutic model to assist this, and the two-way counsellor-client relationship is the focus. Life-coaching intends to pursue a proactive take-and-make approach designed to put together a better whole-life-package than the one in hand, and the 3-way focus is the person, the life-coach and the life. There is certainly overlap between all three, in that a person comes with a multi-dimensional life, whichever door he or she takes. The question then is, What are they looking for, and from whom? In ancient times, of course, distinctions between disciplines were fewer. The healer and medicine-man was also the spiritual one …

8. Vest, Norvene (ed), *Still Listening – New Horizons in Spiritual Direction* (Morehouse Publishing) 2000, pp 100-101.

Where should I meet my directee?

The first thought must always be for the good of the directee. What does he/she need? Privacy would surely be a first, followed by practical considerations around access, and adjacent toilet facilities. Privacy means that your directee is not expecting to meet her/his own community/diocesan/family members on the stairs, no matter how comfortable and welcoming the room at the top. Hence the advantage of one's 'own door' with private access, especially if the place for meeting is a community house or similar.

What about a hotel?

This may have been more commonplace in the past, and if it has changed, this is perhaps more about the understanding of process than change of content. While some people will have found they were able to talk about their prayer life, or just life, over a meal, for many this would not be satisfactory. The power of the Spirit to be present anywhere, anyplace notwithstanding, the 'social setting' does not seem to provide the 'recollecting space' it is the directee's right to expect in a professional relationship. An exception may have to be made for an emergency 'check-in', or if travel precludes the usual setting, but as a regular working place, while a hotel may appear comfortably 'normal,' it does have the potential for distraction, not least that of being swooped upon by a recognising friend. Basically it lacks the consistency of 'own chair own place' in which someone is free to relax, laugh or cry unobserved.

> Directors do not create relationships between God and their
> directees; they try to foster such relationships.[9]

Is there a best way to set up the spiritual direction room?

Your room will be sacred space, so it should offer a sense of spaciousness, even if its actual dimensions are relatively small. The

9. Barry, William A, & Connolly, William J, *The Practice of Spiritual Direction*, (Harper & Row) 1982, p 31.

first necessity is two chairs, and an additional chair if practicable, can offer a choice. Hard, or easy. Everyone has their own sense of what a comfortable inter-personal distance is, and this will dictate how you arrange the chairs. Ideally you can be flexible here, provided the chairs are not so heavy that they are immovable.

As far as décor and decoration go, this is a shared, professional space, and as such, simplicity may be best. Neutral shades are kinder on the eye than vibrant colour and clashing designs. Your own preferences will be evident, but not so strongly as to inhibit a directee's freedom of expression. Alongside any religious symbols, of which one or two may be sufficient, there is always place for pictures or posters of nature, a growing plant or small indoor tree perhaps, and a mirror. The latter being good for light, spaciousness and, more practically, if someone wants to check they 'look all right'.

Is it necessary to have a glass panel in the door of my spiritual direction room?
What is customary in your place of work? Certainly to meet any health or safety requirements, it is necessary to do whatever will model best practice. If you do have a glass panel, or glass door, your chair would face the door, allowing privacy to your directee.

What about sound-proofing?
In times past, buildings were solid, rooms large, and doors oak. Unless this applies to your situation, I believe some form of soundproofing is important in terms of respect for privacy. Solid chipboard nailed to one side of a door, over a commercially produced fibre filling, can help, but if not, a CD of the sounds of the sea, or similar, outside the room, provides a background of white-sound.

What would normally be talked about when 'contracting' with a new directee?
With names and numbers exchanged, a contract, written or

spoken, sets out a mutually agreed position, and normally covers the aspects of place, time and frequency of meeting. Also, what the expectations are, from the space and of the director, how many sessions before a time of evaluation, (perhaps six meetings) and an agreement around remuneration.

How do I best prepare for a session?
I believe it is important to come with a receptive heart; open to God, open to the other. To be calm and, as far as this is possible, relatively uncluttered.

If you keep notes, you will have them to hand somewhere for yourself, reminding you of salient points from last time. Hopefully you will be able to have some moments, bringing the person and your meeting into prayer. A Bible is at hand, and the room is ready. If you have a candle, do you light it before, or do you prefer to do that once the person is seated? You may have agreed on an opening prayer, or ritual.

Am I the one supposed to think of scripture texts?
This is a question I remember hearing at a first training programme many years ago and there was anxiety in the speaker's voice. Perhaps it is reassuring to bear in mind that ultimately, those who are seeking God will find His Guidance either with us, or in spite of us. We have probably had our own experience in, say, a directed retreat, when we might have taken down a text 'wrongly' and yet it turns out to be the one most deeply embued with God's word to us. So it does not all lie in our hands.

As spiritual directors, we need to be careful not to impose our theological resolutions or positions on our directees. When directees describe a theological approach very different from our own, we may need to work with our affective responses so that they do not get in the way of directees' meaning-making process. We need to pay attention in supervision to theological conflicts of interpretation as well as our counter-transference reactions. By reflecting on our strong reactions, we learn to plant seeds and open possibilities to our directees without imposing our own views.[10]

---

10. Rufing, *ibid*, p 86.

So how do I find the 'right' scripture text?

All you can do is offer, and then step back. The annotated selection of texts presented here, some in truncated form, but intended
for the directee's reading and reflection in full, from a Bible,
could easily be annotated differently. As such it is about the
mystery of heart meeting Word, and finding Heart. As a director, you may have heard human 'themes'coming up (conflict,
loss, gratitude etc) and with more or less familiarity in your
heart, or using a concordance, or this book or another, you will
connect these themes with specific texts. You may not be always
'right' of course, but you will be offering a sincerely intuited
suggestion which, given and received in good faith, then allows
the Spirit to do the rest.

Many texts or just one?

I think it is important to check whether someone likes several
texts to pray with (whether in direction, or in a retreat), or
prefers to spend a month on one text. Let us respect this, especially if the person has experience and wisdom on their side.

> If directors do help directees to pay attention to the Lord, they find
> that the simple act of looking at the Lord in a scriptural event, or in
> some other event or situation, is in itself productive prayer. This con-
> templation produces, all by itself, sprouts of love, affection and
> desire; and these in turn lead the person to look more closely at the
> Lord.[11]

I feel so inadequate.

Excellent! As an existential stance, this leaves so much more
room for the Spirit and the individual. I've always found reassurance in the words, attributed to St Basil: 'When you have
become His, in the measure that He decides, then He will know
how to bestow you on others.' They say humility is truth. This
puts the responsibility firmly where it really lies.

---

11. Connolly, *ibid*, p 59.

What if I feel lost in a session?

Someone once shared, with rueful hindsight, 'Although I felt lost during that session, at no time did I ask God for help!' Perhaps it also helps to do as one might when feeling lost on a walk. Stand still, notice what you recognise, and start from there, or retrace to the point where you last knew where you were. No harm in checking that you and the directee are in the same country.

Suppose 'nothing is happening'?

What are we expecting to happen? Perhaps we need to check with ourselves. 'Is this my own anxiety? Is this my own impatience? Do I feel I should be 'performing better' here? (Not our role.) Am I looking further down the road, and wanting to urge my directee to 'hurry up' and see what I see?' (Not appropriate). Either way, perhaps we simply need to re-engage our focus with the directee, and what they are feeling (ask) and then together we may notice where energy is alive, smothered, or re-orientated. What does their life look like at this moment, both in content and in body-mind-spirit schedules. Then we take it from this present moment, the 'Now'.

> I encourage directees to make time for prayer and for solitude by scheduling it just as they would schedule any other appointment of their professional or private life.[12]

Is it appropriate to share one's own spiritual orientation?

Someone once told me that she had presented her own position on a topic, and that the person she spoke to felt 'too influenced' to continue. Returning a question to the speaker may be better than presenting a teaching. Another director tells me he stated, 'While as a Christian I cannot agree with this position, nevertheless, I support you, and please feel free to come back.' Which the person did. As far as denomination is concerned, one would ex-

---

12. Cashman, *ibid*, p 12.

pect that a potential directee will have enquired as to the religious tradition of a potential director. This should be clarified.

Should I say it, if I am a religious? A priest?
Why not? This is spiritual direction. Somehow, people tend to know, anyway.

Are there any 'no-go' areas regarding what is talked about?
Is this a contract which concerns itself specifically with what occurs during prayer times – as perhaps on a directed retreat? Or is the agreement about life *per se*, and exploring God's working in that? In the latter, the arena may appear broader, but ultimately, you will still be listening for the *theme* within the story, and how wide and deep you go with that, depends on your sensitivity, training, and parameters. One rule of thumb might be, 'Don't open what you feel you can't close.' Which for me means, 'Stay within the brief of our agreement and (if I can dare use the word) my expertise.' Referral is always an option and for this reason, it is important to have at hand a number of respected colleagues, in the addiction, medical, psychological and stress-management support areas.

> The spiritual director one has the enormous privilege of seeing the interaction between God and another human being. There is no other relationship that has that encounter as its explicit aim.[13]

Do sessions stop with the directee just not re-appearing? And am I supposed to ring them about missed appointments?
Perhaps this all depends on what you have both agreed in the initial contracting. It certainly is easier for a directee to know they can bow out gracefully, if they wish, after an agreed number of 'lets-see-how-we-get-on' sessions. It would be customary to let the 'final' agreed session include some mutual evaluation, after which the meetings end, or continue on at agreed intervals.

13. Margaret A. L. Blackie, *ibid*, p 30.

As to ringing to find out why someone hasn't re-appeared, I myself do not ring up, but I believe some directors do. Choice.

If someone wants to leave after twenty-five minutes, is it necessary to sit out a whole hour?
What has been happening during the session? What is the 'flavour' of the leaving? Basically, you offer the space, the person is free to use it. The 'fifty-minute' hour has usually seemed good, but time can be negotiated. What may be more important is that last word which they leave with you before they go.

What about lateness?
I like to believe in peoples' basic integrity, and that there is a real reason (traffic, meetings etc) for coming late. Here are normally responsible adults. I find lateness relatively rare, and when it happens, the time is held. I stay put for at least half an hour, and if I can accommodate a few extra minutes afterwards, I like to do that too. If lateness would occur regularly, I simply enquire if a different time might suit the individual better.[14]

Are there any questions I could/should be asking myself after a session?
I am replying with the words someone passed on to me from her own practice: Where was God in this meeting? How was I myself challenged, stretched, disturbed?' You may have similar questions … As both have listened, what images are coming up, perhaps from dreams? What patterns are we both noticing? Are any questions emerging? What notes do I need to make?

> Each spiritual director needs companionship on his or her own spiritual journey, a spiritual director. And each spiritual director needs a companion on his or her journey as spiritual director, a supervisor, or supervision group. *Blackie*

---

14. In a situation where regular meetings are weekly or fortnightly – as in counselling – persistent lateness might relate to reluctance around some aspect of the process, but such in-depth attribution would not necessarily apply here, in spiritual direction.

Is supervision really necessary for spiritual directors, or is it just something we have inherited from counselling practice?

Since human beings are equally precious and potentially vulnerable in any relationship of self-disclosure, whatever the content, it is primarily for the well-being of directees that a measure of accountability is entirely appropriate for spiritual directors. Apart from the safety aspect, supervision allows spiritual directors to connect with their own responses, including possible occasions of counter-transference. It allows for reflection on best practice and evaluation of how this is being effective, and if not, why not, and where to go from there.

Alongside that, reflection on scripture, the mystical tradition and contemporary spiritual writing, hopefully keeps us awake to our named Christian values and where, if and how we actually 'walk the talk'.

How can I respect confidentiality and talk about the person in supervision?

Supervision is about the director's process, not a replay of the directee's issues or prayer-life, so provided that is borne in mind, confidentiality remains intact. However, since it is often easier to talk about someone other than oneself, self-avoidance needs to be borne in mind as well. So personal reflection before supervision will give you the 'story' – then we can go behind that and observe yourself, how was I, what did I feel, e.g. 'When my directee (unnamed of course) mentioned the word 'mother' I felt I wanted to cry.' (Is there something unresolved in my life here?) 'When my directee said she thought it was time to find a new director, I felt angry and resentful …' So it is about tracking what and when, rather than telling all, because the 'all' may not be where the relevance is.

What support is available to me out there in my work as a spiritual director?

Wherever you trained, there will hopefully be someone or two with whom you might choose to meet occasionally for peer support. You are also likely to find the current courses do offer on-going support, in terms of group supervision, and the informal connection that accompanies the space. There are accrediting bodies, like AISGA (All Ireland Spiritual Guidance Association, (Details in appendix), and the spiritual arm of BACP (British Association of Counselling and Psychotherapy). Heart-Works (Grace Dieu, Waterford) and An Croí (Asdhbourne, Co Meath) offer ways of ongoing support, in-service courses, and group supervision, and there is the international network of Spiritual Directors International, USA, with its networking publications and website. (Details in Appendix)

> Present-day directors do not give answers or tell directees what to do in their relationship with God or when making life-ch oices. Instead, they listen with directees for how the Spirit of God is present and active.[15]

Do gender issues impact on spiritual direction?
It is now widely accepted that men and women operate out of differing frames of reference, and that they will use different modes of communicating their experience, and no less their spiritual experience. A director would need to be aware of this, and comfortable with different modalities – discourse, dreams, imagery etc. It is equally important for the director to be aware of any latent prejudices or fears regarding gender, and address these in his/her own personal work, especially if he/she is intending to accompany the whole spectrum of humanity.

Any suggestions that might help the directee engage with their process?
Outside a session, your directee will be getting on with their life, and within that, the process is of seeking and finding God in all things, and oneself in God. How to help this? One way is to develop the practice of saying 'Thank-you' when something comes up that delights. Another way is to practise specific attention to the four common experiences of beauty, ugliness, pleasure, and

---

15. Bakke, *ibid*, p 19.

pain and spontaneously pray out of these.[16] Writing out, and praying with dreams, painting and drawing images in one's prayer-experience can hold attention, and where scripture is concerned, the use of a scripture-commentary, while sounding too academic to some initially, has often proved helpful in terms of 'getting into' a text, and its context.[17]

My directees always go over time, even when I need to finish at a specific time. What can I do?

Basically, remember that it is your brief to watch time, not the responsibility of the directee, who needs to feel free. So a director needs to develop a sense of the overall form and pace of a session, and gauge when it is time to start the re-entry to cars and traffic, to which your directee will return in a few minutes. Practice makes this natural, but some general tips are: Not taking on a new topic ten minutes before closure, (but remembering last words, for next time), introducing the arrangements for the next meeting, taking up your diary, gently beginning withdrawal of total eye-contact and energy focus, slightly shifting position, and sometimes even standing up, or shaking hands. The above body-language can help if you find it difficult to actually say something specific like, 'Well, I'm afraid we are coming to the end of our time, and we might look at dates for the next time'etc. (Of course there will be occasional exceptions to the above, where sensitivity and concern need to take precedence over a clock).

How do I take care of myself or 'wind down' after a session?

In order to disperse any excess of adrenaline, notice how you feel, headline your notes, breathe deeply a few times, walk around, do some stretches, notice how you feel, and give yourself some

---

16. For this point, used and adapted since the 1980s, I am indebted to Fr John Edwards SJ, London.

17. Though 'dated' William Barclay's reprinted commentaries combine reflection and fact which can help engage someone without a scripture background.

quiet moments, with closed eyes, to come back to yourself, and then or later, perhaps journal or extend your notes.

Is it advisable to change spiritual directors after a couple of years or is it okay to stay with the same one for the long haul?
There is no real precedent here, as reading the lives of different European mystics shows, where director was confessor and there might be more than one over years, although one was often related to as 'chief confessor.'[18]

In spiritual direction, perhaps the question for a directee might be on the lines of, 'Am I getting what I am looking for in terms of support? Do I feel I am moving (which does not mean speeding) forward in my spiritual life? Do I feel the connection is fresh or stale? What does this mean for me?

> Spiritual directors with a good deal of personal experience of prayer, know they are entering on holy ground and that they do so with at least some fear and trembling. It is right that they be in awe and afraid that they might falter and fail the directee. Such feelings … are realistic and appropriate and do not incapacitate them.[19]

Should spiritual directors, once they have had a first session, ever let a directee go?
A trial-period with a new directee can be a good idea. This allows a director as well as a directee to sense whether this connection is right for both all round, and to terminate without long explanation. 'After our four meetings, I feel that I am not really the person for you, and I can suggest …' While sensitivity, care and courtesy are uppermost here, honesty with oneself is very important, as a learning. What is stopping me wholeheartedly accompanying this person?'

The reasons may be time-pressure, greater needs than you are professionally able to handle, a counter-transference that blocks you, close family or community ties making confidentiality

---

18. Cf Catherine of Siena or Teresa of Avila.
19. Connolly, *ibid*, p 128.

a problem, a racial or sexual prejudice, a 'gut' feeling, very different spiritual positions. With a long-established directee, it is still good to evaluate from time to time, perhaps after a summer break. Usually a 'moving-on' has already been 'in the air' and is mutuality understood, and accepted as the next best step.

What if there came a time when I may have to acknowledge that I can no longer be in a position of director, due to perceived difficulties in the relationship? If so, how do I approach it?
One would hope that, in a situation like this, the relationship would have been monitored all along the way, rather than precipitate a sudden crisis, and that a separation would be prepared for and amicable. Since it is important that a directee, like anyone in a pastoral or therapeutic relationship, should not feel suddenly 'abandoned', such a move on the director's part would need to be maturely and sensitively handled. How much and what you say to the directee would depend on the nature of the relationship. Is this about faith, sex, feeling incompetent, active dislike (counter-transference)? 'Difficulties' can also be a doorway to growth, so it would be useful to discuss your position with your supervisor, before just pulling out unilaterally.

Where does money come in, if at all?
Lack of or limited funds should never preclude anyone from spiritual direction, and some flexibility will occur around this. Current thinking around renumeration is that some agreed exchange is important, valuing the ministry, and respecting both the directee and the director's circumstances.

Are there any training courses available, with the possibility of accreditation?
See appendix for Irish spiritual-direction training courses.

Is there any specific way of making a session-evaluation?
Each director will have their own way of holding the sessions and their directees in mind and heart, so if I offer a simple sug-

gestion of my own. It might prove a short but salient support for those who are starting out without yet any particular format to hand ... It is of course, infinitely adaptable. (See box below.)

Who comes for spiritual direction? Mainly religious?
Mainly but not only. As far back as the days of the Desert Fathers and Mothers in Egypt, seekers after a deeper spiritual life have sought out a mentor or spiritual companion. This became more formalised with the establishment of monasteries, and a specifically-dedicated religious life, but lay singles and marrieds are both mentioned as spiritual directees throughout much of the Christian tradition, as well as clergy, members of religious orders whether in community or single-living, women or men. This is happening again now, with websites, wide availability of theology and spirituality courses, books, and by-product media encouragement. With maybe different contexts, but not necessarily different expectations, the spectrum for spiritual accompaniment is widening. Let us pray to be open, gracious and respectful to the call of the Spirit.

Session-Evaluation

Person: (Name).

Priorities: (What came up as significant?)

Process: (Where / how was I aware of this?)

Pace: (Was I able to stay with the directee's pace?)

Progression: (In which direction did the session move?

    Where are we now?)

Points: (To remember for next time)

Problems: (Experienced in myself, or by the directee)

Prayer: (What is my own prayer here?)

FOR JOURNALLING AND REFLECTION

Personal Faith Journey

Who or what first told me or showed me the presence of God?

What were the significant God-moments in my childhood?

Who was God in my prayer?

Looking back as an adult on my first 25 years, what
were the hills and valleys, oases and deserts?

What brought me nourishment? What filled my well?

Who was my God? How did I pray?

Looking back over my post-25 year stage up until now,
what are the significant spiritual shifts that I have
experienced, and what occasioned these?

How did these change my sense of God?

What is my present prayer practice, and what means
do I have of living out a holistic spiritual life?

Where am I going?

What am I being asked to let go of?

Where do I feel called?

Creative Expression for Directees or Retreatants

If I were to image myself in paint or crayon, what would that be?

If I were to create a mandala of my life at this time, indicating
what is behind me, alongside me and what I sense is ahead of
me, what would it look like in terms of symbol?[20]

How can I best set up a prayer-space that speaks to me of
God?

What music am I listening to? How is this deepening my
spiritual life?

---

20. A pictorial symbol, usually a circle within a square, often with four
motifs, around a centre, used as an aid to reflection, meditation.

Texts

Spiritual-Life Themes

— *Change and Transition* —

Needing to   Jeremiah 29:11-13
find hope in   ¹¹'For surely I know the plans
the future   I have for you,' says the Lord,
                 'plans for your welfare and not for harm,
                 to give you a future with hope.
                 ¹²Then when you call upon me
                 and come and pray to me, I will hear you.
                 ¹³When you search for me, you will find me;
                 if you seek me with all your heart,

Time to   Luke 2:19
discern   ¹⁹But Mary treasured all these words
                 and pondered them in her heart.

Taking the   Ecclesiastes 3:1-4ff
next step   ¹For everything there is a season,
                 and a time for every matter under heaven:
                 ²a time to be born, and a time to die;
                 a time to plant, and a time to pluck up what is planted;
                 ³a time to kill, and a time to heal;
                 a time to break down, and a time to build up;
                 ⁴a time to weep, and a time to laugh;
                 a time to mourn, and a time to dance;

Experiencing   2 Cor 1:17-20
ambivalence   ¹⁷Was I vacillating
                 when I wanted to do this?
                 Do I make my plans
                 according to ordinary human standards,
                 ready to say 'Yes, yes'
                 and 'No, no' at the same time?
                 ¹⁸As surely as God is faithful,

our word to you has not been 'Yes and No.'
[19]For the Son of God, Jesus Christ,
whom we proclaimed among you,
Silvanus and Timothy and I,
was not 'Yes and No';
but in him it is always 'Yes.'
[20]For in him
every one of God's promises is a 'Yes.'

Gen 28:10, 12, 16-17   *Noticing*
[10]Jacob left Beer-sheba …   *God in this*
[12]And he dreamed   *present place*
that there was a ladder
set up on the earth, the top of it
reaching to heaven;
and the angels of God
were ascending
and descending on it.
[16]Then Jacob woke from his sleep
and said, 'Surely the Lord is in this place
– and I did not know it!'
[17]And he was afraid, and said,
'How awesome is this place!
This is none other than the house of God,
and this is the gate of heaven.'

Psalm 102:24-27   *Coming to*
[24] 'O my God,' I say,   *terms with*
'do not take me away   *endings*
at the mid-point of my life,
you whose years endure
throughout all generations.
[25]Long ago you laid
the foundation of the earth,
and the heavens are the work of your hands.
[26]They will perish, but you endure;

they will all wear out like a garment.
You change them like clothing,
and they pass away;
27but you are the same, and your years have no end.

Reframing   *John 16:7-11ff*
7Nevertheless I tell you the truth:
it is to your advantage that I go away,
for if I do not go away,
the Advocate will not come to you;
but if I go, I will send him to you.
8And when he comes,
he will prove the world wrong about sin
and righteousness and judgment:
9about sin, because they do not believe in me;
10about righteousness,
because I am going to the Father
and you will see me no longer;
11about judgment,
because the ruler of this world
has been condemned.

When every-   *Isaiah 54:10ff*
thing seems   10For the mountains may depart
different   and the hills be removed,
but my steadfast love
shall not depart from you,
and my covenant of peace
shall not be removed, says the Lord,
who has compassion on you.

Where am I   *Gen 16:7-9ff*
going?   7The angel of the Lord
found her by a spring of water
in the wilderness …
the spring on the way to Shur.

8And he said, 'Hagar, slave-girl of Sarai,
where have you come from
and where are you going?'
She said,
'I am running away
from my mistress Sarai.'

— Coming to terms with the past —

Jonah 2:3-7ff   *Telling the*
3You cast me into the deep,   *story*
into the heart of the seas,
and the flood surrounded me;
all your waves and your billows passed over me.
4Then I said, 'I am driven away
from your sight;
how shall I look again
upon your holy temple?'
5The waters closed in over me;
the deep surrounded me;
weeds were wrapped around my head
6at the roots of the mountains.
I went down to the land
whose bars closed upon me forever;
yet you brought up my life from the Pit,
O Lord my God.
7As my life was ebbing away,
I remembered the Lord;
and my prayer came to you, into your holy temple.

Ezekiel 36:26-27ff   *When I can't*
26A new heart I will give you,   *make it alone*
and a new spirit I will put within you;
and I will remove from your body
the heart of stone and give you
a heart of flesh.

Finding
meaning
once more

Isaiah 54:4-8

4Do not fear, for you will not be ashamed;
do not be discouraged,
for you will not suffer disgrace;
for you will forget the shame of your youth,
and the disgrace of your widowhood
you will remember no more.
5For your Maker is your husband,
the Lord of hosts is his name;
the Holy One of Israel is your Redeemer,
the God of the whole earth he is called.
6For the Lord has called you
like a wife forsaken and grieved in spirit,
like the wife of a man's youth when she is cast off,
says your God.
7For a brief moment I abandoned you,
but with great compassion I will gather you.
8In overflowing wrath for a moment
I hid my face from you,
but with everlasting love
I will have compassion on you,
says the Lord, your Redeemer.

Receiving
peace as a
gift

John 14:27

27Peace I leave with you;
my peace I give to you.
I do not give to you as the world gives.
Do not let your hearts be troubled,
and do not let them be afraid.

Reconnecting
with the
Source

Colossians 1:11-14

11May you be made strong
with all the strength
that comes from his glorious power,
and may you be prepared to endure
everything with patience,

while joyfully
¹²giving thanks to the Father,
who has enabled you to share in the inheritance
of the saints in the light.
¹³He has rescued us from the power of darkness
and transferred us into the kingdom of his beloved Son,
¹⁴in whom we have redemption, the forgiveness of sins.

2 Cor 5:17ff   *Moving on*
¹⁷So if anyone is in Christ,
there is a new creation:
everything old has passed away;
see, everything has become new!

— *Conflict* —

Gen 32:24-26ff   *Struggling*
²⁴Jacob was left alone;   *with true*
and a man   *and false self*
wrestled with him until daybreak.
²⁵When the man saw
that he did not prevail against Jacob,
he struck him on the hip socket;
and Jacob's hip was put out of joint
as he wrestled with him.
²⁶Then he said,
'Let me go, for the day is breaking.'

Mark 10:17, 21-22ff   *Struggling*
¹⁷As he was setting out on a journey,   *with*
a man ran up and knelt before him,   *attachment*
and asked him,
'Good Teacher,
what must I do to inherit eternal life?'
²¹Jesus, looking at him, loved him and said,
'You lack one thing;

go, sell what you own,
and give the money to the poor,
and you will have treasure in heaven;
then come, follow me.'
22When he heard this, he was shocked
and went away grieving, for he had many possessions.

Divided
loyalties

Luke 8:27-30
27As he stepped out on land,
a man of the city
who had demons met him.
For a long time he had worn no clothes,
and he did not live in a house but in the tombs.
28When he saw Jesus,
he fell down before him
and shouted at the top of his voice,
'What have you to do with me,
Jesus, Son of the Most High God?
I beg you, do not torment me' –
29for Jesus had commanded the unclean spirit
to come out of the man.
(For many times it had seized him;
he was kept under guard
and bound with chains and shackles,
but he would break the bonds
and be driven by the demon into the wilds.)
30Jesus then asked him, 'What is your name?'

Tempted to
misuse
power and
gifts

Luke 4:1-4ff
1Jesus, full of the Holy Spirit,
returned from the Jordan
and was led by the Spirit
in the wilderness,
2where for forty days
he was tempted by the devil.
He ate nothing at all during those days,

and when they were over, he was famished.
³The devil said to him,
'If you are the Son of God,
command this stone
to become a loaf of bread.'
⁴Jesus answered him,
'It is written,
"One does not live by bread alone".'

Ephesians 6:10-16ff

Finally, be strong in the Lord
and in the strength of his power.
¹¹Put on the whole armour of God,
so that you may be able to stand
against the wiles of the devil.
¹³Therefore take up the whole armour of God.
¹⁴Stand therefore,
and fasten the belt of truth
around your waist,
and put on the breastplate
of righteousness.
¹⁵As shoes for your feet
put on whatever
will make you ready
to proclaim the gospel of peace.
¹⁶With all of these,
take the shield of faith.

When needing spiritual protection

Psalm 121:1-8

¹I lift up my eyes to the hills –
from where will my help come?
²My help comes from the Lord,
who made heaven and earth.
³He will not let your foot be moved;
he who keeps you will not slumber.

Seeking the source of help

[4]He who keeps Israel
will neither slumber nor sleep.
[5]The Lord is your keeper;
the Lord is your shade at your right hand.
[6]The sun shall not strike you by day,
nor the moon by night.
[7]The Lord will keep you from all evil;
he will keep your life.
[8]The Lord will keep
your going out and your coming in
from this time on and forevermore.

— *Connecting with Creation* —

Finding the Creator in creation

Psalm 65:6-13ff
[6]By your strength
you established the mountains;
you are girded with might.
[7]You silence the roaring of the seas,
the roaring of their waves,
the tumult of the peoples.
[8]Those who live at earth's farthest bounds
are awed by your signs;
you make the gateways of the
morning and the evening shout for joy.
[9]You visit the earth and water it,
you greatly enrich it;
the river of God is full of water;
you provide the people with grain,
for so you have prepared it.
[10]You water its furrows abundantly,
settling its ridges,
softening it with showers,
and blessing its growth.
[11]You crown the year with your bounty;
your wagon tracks overflow with richness.

[12]The pastures of the wilderness overflow,
the hills gird themselves with joy,
[13]the meadows clothe themselves with flocks,
the valleys deck themselves with grain,
they shout and sing together for joy.

Job 39:26-29ff   *Limits of*
'Is it by your wisdom   *knowledge*
that the hawk soars,
and spreads its wings toward the south?
[27]Is it at your command
that the eagle mounts up
and makes its nest on high?
[28]It lives on the rock
and makes its home
in the fastness of the rocky crag.
[29]From there it spies the prey;
its eyes see it from far away.

Gen 1:1-5, 8-10ff   *Inter-*
[1]In the beginning   *connectedness*
when God created the heavens and the earth,
[2]the earth was a formless void
and darkness covered the face of the deep,
while a wind from God
swept over the face of the waters.
[3]Then God said,'Let there be light';
and there was light.
[4]And God saw that the light was good;
and God separated the light from the darkness.
[5]God called the light Day,
and the darkness he called Night.
[8]God called the dome Sky.
[10]God called the dry land Earth,
And God saw that it was good.

Sensing the
Creator's
call to life
within
Creation
and in my
own body,
mind and
spirit

Romans 8:19-23

[19]For the creation waits with eager longing
for the revealing of the children of God;
[20]for the creation was subjected to futility,
not of its own will but by the will of the one
who subjected it, in hope
[21]that the creation itself will be set free
from its bondage to decay
and will obtain the freedom
of the glory of the children of God.
[22]We know that the whole creation
has been groaning in labour pains until now;
[23]and not only the creation,
but we ourselves, who have the first fruits of the Spirit,
groan inwardly while we wait for adoption,
the redemption of our bodies.

Learning
from nature

Luke 12:24-26ff

[24]Consider the ravens:
they neither sow nor reap,
they have neither storehouse nor barn,
and yet God feeds them.
Of how much more value are you
than the birds!
[25]And can any of you by worrying
add a single hour to your span of life?
[26]If then you are not able to do
so small a thing as that,
why do you worry about the rest?

Noticing
life's cycles

Psalm 19:1-6 ff

[1]The heavens are telling the glory of God;
and the firmament proclaims his handiwork.
[2]Day to day pours forth speech,
and night to night declares knowledge.

[3]There is no speech, nor are there words;
their voice is not heard;
[4]yet their voice goes out through all the earth,
and their words to the end of the world.
In the heavens he has set a tent for the sun,
[5]which comes out like a bridegroom
from his wedding canopy,
and like a strong man runs its course with joy.
[6]Its rising is from the end of the heavens,
and its circuit to the end of them;
and nothing is hid from its heat.

Psalm 8   *A sense of*
[1]O Lord, our Sovereign,   *wonder*
how majestic is your name in all the earth!   *and awe*
You have set your glory above the heavens.
[2]Out of the mouths of babes and infants
you have founded a bulwark
because of your foes,
to silence the enemy and the avenger.
[3]When I look at your heavens,
the work of your fingers,
the moon and the stars
that you have established;
[4]what are human beings
that you are mindful of them,
mortals that you care for them?

— *Deepening Spiritual Life* —

Creating   *Rev 3:20*
inner space   Listen! I am standing at the door,
                knocking;
                if you hear my voice and open the door,
                I will come in to you
                and eat with you, and you with me.

Committing   *Ezekiel 36:27-28*
to spiritual 27I will put my spirit within you,
practice   and make you follow my statutes
                and be careful to observe my ordinances.
                28Then you shall live in the land
                that I gave to your ancestors;
                and you shall be my people,
                and I will be your God.

Making   *Genesis 12:1-2ff*
the break   1Now the Lord said to Abram,
                'Go from your country
                and your kindred and your father's house
                to the land that I will show you.
                2I will make of you a great nation,
                and I will bless you,
                and make your name great,
                so that you will be a blessing.'

Seeing with   *John 3:1-4ff*
new eyes   1Now there was a Pharisee
                named Nicodemus, a leader of the Jews.
                2He came to Jesus by night
                and said to him,
                'Rabbi, we know that you are a teacher
                who has come from God;

for no one can do these signs
that you do apart from the presence of God.'
3Jesus answered him,
'Very truly, I tell you,
no one can see the kingdom of God
without being born from above.'
4Nicodemus said to him,
'How can anyone be born
after having grown old?

Isaiah 55:1-3ff   *Deepening*
1Ho, everyone who thirsts,   *ways of*
come to the waters;   *prayer*
and you that have no money,
come, buy and eat!
Come, buy wine and milk
without money and without price.
2Why do you spend your money
for that which is not bread,
and your labour for that which does not satisfy?
Listen carefully to me,
and eat what is good,
and delight yourselves in rich food.
3Incline your ear, and come to me;
listen, so that you may live.

Luke 8:43-48   *Allowing*
43Now there was a woman   *vulnerability*
who had been suffering
from haemorrhages
for twelve years;
and though she had spent all she had on physicians,
no one could cure her.
44She came up behind him
and touched the fringe of his clothes,
and immediately her haemorrhage stopped.

45Then Jesus asked,'Who touched me?'
When all denied it, Peter said,
'Master, the crowds surround you and press in on you.'
46But Jesus said,'Someone touched me;
for I noticed that power had gone out from me.'
47When the woman saw
that she could not remain hidden,
she came trembling; and falling down before him,
she declared in the presence of all the people
why she had touched him,
and how she had been immediately healed.
48He said to her,
'Daughter, your faith has made you well; go in peace.'

Longing for   Psalm 63:1-8
deeper   1O God, you are my God, I seek you,
intimacy   my soul thirsts for you;
                my flesh faints for you,
                as in a dry and weary land
                where there is no water.
                2So I have looked upon you
                in the sanctuary,
                beholding your power and glory.
                3Because your steadfast love
                is better than life,
                my lips will praise you.
                4So I will bless you as long as I live;
                I will lift up my hands and call on your name.
                5My soul is satisfied as with a rich feast,
                and my mouth praises you with joyful lips
                6when I think of you on my bed,
                and meditate on you in the watches of the night;
                7for you have been my help,
                and in the shadow of your wings I sing for joy.
                8My soul clings to you;
                your right hand upholds me.

Song of Songs 2:8-12, 16   *Letting*
⁸The voice of my beloved!   *love in*
Look, he comes, leaping upon the mountains,
bounding over the hills.
⁹My beloved is like a gazelle
or a young stag.
Look, there he stands behind our wall,
gazing in at the windows, looking through the lattice.
¹⁰My beloved speaks and says to me:
'Arise, my love, my fair one, and come away;
¹¹for now the winter is past, the rain is over and gone.
¹²The flowers appear on the earth;
the time of singing has come …
and the voice of the turtledove is heard in our land.
¹⁶My beloved is mine and I am his;
he pastures his flock among the lilies.

Ephesians 1:3ff   *Remembering*
³Blessed be the God   *personal*
and Father of our Lord Jesus Christ,   *blessings*
who has blessed us in Christ
with every spiritual blessing
in the heavenly places.

Luke 1:26-28, 38   *Saying 'yes'*
²⁶In the sixth month the angel Gabrielwas sent by God
to a town in Galilee called Nazareth,
²⁷to a virgin engaged to a man
whose name was Joseph,
of the house of David.
The virgin's name was Mary.
²⁸And he came to her and said,
'Greetings, favoured one! The Lord is with you.'
³⁸Then Mary said,'Here am I, the servant of the Lord;
let it be with me according to your word.'
Then the angel departed from her.

Dropping
the masks

Matthew 18:1-5

[1]At that time the disciples came to Jesus and asked,
'Who is the greatest in the kingdom of heaven?'
[2]He called a child, whom he put among them,
[3]and said,'Truly I tell you,
unless you change
and become like children,
you will never enter
the kingdom of heaven.
[4]Whoever becomes humble like this child
is the greatest in the kingdom of heaven.
[5]Whoever welcomes one such child in my name
welcomes me.

— *Depths of Pain* —

Betrayal

Psalm 55,4-5, 12-14ff

[4]My heart is in anguish within me,
the terrors of death have fallen upon me.
[5]Fear and trembling come upon me,
and horror overwhelms me.
[12]It is not enemies who taunt me –
I could bear that;
it is not adversaries who deal insolently with me –
I could hide from them.
[13]But it is you, my equal,
my companion, my familiar friend,
[14]with whom I kept pleasant company;
we walked in the house of God with the throng.

Facing
ultimate
loss

Luke 22: 40-46

[40]When he reached the place, he said to them,
'Pray that you may not come into the time of trial.'
[41]Then he withdrew from them about a stone's throw,
knelt down, and prayed,

[42]'Father, if you are willing,
remove this cup from me;
yet, not my will but yours be done.'
[43]Then an angel from heaven appeared to him
and gave him strength.
[44]In his anguish he prayed more earnestly,
and his sweat became like great drops of blood
falling down on the ground.
[45]When he got up from prayer,
he came to the disciples
and found them sleeping because of grief,
[46]and he said to them,
'Why are you sleeping?
Get up and pray
that you may not come into the time of trial.'

Genesis 21:14-17

*When life's
meaning
ebbs*

[14]And she departed, and wandered about
in the wilderness of Beer-sheba.
[15]When the water in the skin was gone,
she cast the child under one of the bushes.
[16]Then she went and sat down opposite him
a good way off, about the distance of a bowshot;
for she said,'Do not let me look
on the death of the child.'
And as she sat opposite him,
she lifted up her voice and wept.
[17]And God heard the voice of the boy;
and the angel of God called to Hagar from heaven,
and said to her,'What troubles you, Hagar?
Do not be afraid;
for God has heard the voice of the boy where he is.

Dying	*Luke 23:44-47ff*
Inside	44It was now about noon,

and darkness came over the whole land
until three in the afternoon,
45while the suns light failed;
and the curtain of the temple was torn in two.
46Then Jesus, crying with a loud voice,
said,'Father, into your hands I commend my spirit.'
Having said this, he breathed his last.
47When the centurion saw what had taken place,
he praised God and said,
'Certainly this man was innocent.'

Looking   *Psalm 139:11-12ff*
beyond the   11If I say,'Surely the darkness shall cover me,
darkness   and the light around me become night,'
12even the darkness is not dark to you;
the night is as bright as the day,
for darkness is as light to you.

Crying out   *1 Samuel 1:11, 14-16ff*
from the   11She was deeply distressed
heart   and prayed to the Lord, and wept bitterly.
14So Eli said to her,
'How long will you make
a drunken spectacle of yourself?
Put away your wine.'
15But Hannah answered,'No, my Lord,
I am a woman deeply troubled;
I have drunk neither wine nor strong drink,
but I have been pouring out my soul before the Lord.
16Do not regard your servant as a worthless woman,
for I have been speaking out of my great anxiety
and vexation all this time.'

Luke 8:22-24

Feeling
endangered

[22]One day he got into a boat with his disciples,
and he said to them,
'Let us go across to the other side of the lake.'
So they put out, [23]and while they were sailing
he fell asleep. A windstorm swept down on the lake,
and the boat was filling with water,
and they were in danger.
[24]They went to him and woke him up, shouting,
'Master, Master, we are perishing!'
And he woke up and rebuked the wind
and the raging waves; they ceased,
and there was a calm.

Luke 2:34-35

Experiencing
helplessness
especially as
a mother

[34]Then Simeon blessed them
and said to his mother Mary,
'This child is destined for the falling
and the rising of many in Israel,
and to be a sign that will be opposed
[35]so that the inner thoughts of many
will be revealed
– and a sword will pierce your own soul too.'

Isaiah 53:3-4

Suffering
alienation
and rejection

[3]He was despised
and rejected by others;
a man of suffering and acquainted with infirmity;
and as one from whom others hide their faces
he was despised, and we held him of no account.
[4]Surely he has borne our infirmities
and carried our diseases;
yet we accounted him stricken,
struck down by God, and afflicted.

Feeling *over-* *whelmed*	*Psalm 69:1-3ff* [1]Save me, O God, for the waters have come up to my neck. [2]I sink in deep mire, where there is no foothold; I have come into deep waters, and the flood sweeps over me. [3]I am weary with my crying; my throat is parched. My eyes grow dim with waiting for my God.
Out of *depths,* *hope*	*Psalm 130:1-6ff* [1]Out of the depths I cry to you, O Lord. [2]Lord, hear my voice! Let your ears be attentive to the voice of my supplications! [3]If you, O Lord, should mark iniquities, Lord, who could stand? [4]But there is forgiveness with you, so that you may be revered. [5]I wait for the Lord, my soul waits, and in his word I hope; [6]my soul waits for the Lord more than those who watch for the morning, more than those who watch for the morning.
Noticing *patterns of* *past care*	*Isaiah 41:8-10* [8]But you, Israel, my servant, Jacob, whom I have chosen, the offspring of Abraham, my friend; [9]you whom I took from the ends of the earth, and called from its farthest corners, saying to you,'You are my servant, I have chosen you and not cast you off';

[10]do not fear, for I am with you,
do not be afraid, for I am your God;
I will strengthen you, I will help you,
I will uphold you with my victorious right hand.

Psalm 43:3-5ff   *Coming*
[3]O send out your light and your truth;   *through*
let them lead me;
let them bring me to your holy hill
and to your dwelling.
[4]Then I will go to the altar of God,
to God my exceeding joy;
and I will praise you with the harp,
O God, my God.
[5]Why are you cast down, O my soul,
and why are you disquieted within me?
Hope in God;
for I shall again praise him,
my help and my God.

— *Dryness* —

Hosea 3:14   *Acknowledging*
I will ... bring her into the wilderness,   *apathy*
and speak to her tenderly there.
There I will give back her
vineyards to her,
and transform
her valley of Troubles
into a Door of Hope.[21]

Ezekiel 37:1-5   *Dried-up —*
[1]The hand of the Lord   *burnt-out*
came upon me,

---

21. *The Living Bible* (Coverdale House Publishers UK, for Tyndale House
Publishers, Illinois, USA. 1971.

and he brought me out
by the spirit of the Lord
and set me down in the middle of a valley;
it was full of bones.
²He led me all around them;
there were very many lying in the valley,
and they were very dry.
³He said to me,'Mortal, can these bones live?'
I answered,'O Lord God, you know.'
⁴Then he said to me,'Prophesy to these bones,
and say to them: O dry bones,
hear the word of the Lord.
⁵Thus says the Lord God to these bones:
I will cause breath to enter you, and you shall live.

Losing   *Luke 24:13-14, 21, 25-29ff*
heart,   ¹³Now on that same day two of them
disillusioned were going to a village called Emmaus,
about seven miles from Jerusalem,
¹⁴and talking with each other
about all these things that had happened.
²¹But we had hoped that he was the one to redeem Israel.
Yes, and besides all this,
it is now the third day since these things took place.
²⁵Then he said to them,'Oh, how foolish you are,
and how slow of heart to believe
all that the prophets have declared!'
²⁸As they came near the village
to which they were going,
he walked ahead as if he were going on.
²⁹But they urged him strongly, saying,
'Stay with us, because it is almost evening
and the day is now nearly over.'
So he went in to stay with them.

Acts 17:27b-28

27bHe is not far from each one of us.
28For 'In him we live and move
and have our being.'

*Wanting to
touch the
Spiritual*

— *Forgiveness* —

Matthew 18:21-22

21Then Peter came and said to him,
'Lord, if another member of the church
sins against me, how often should I forgive?
As many as seven times?'
22Jesus said to him,
'Not seven times,
but, I tell you, seventy-seven times.'

*'Surely
I've done
enough!'*

Psalm 51:1-3ff

1Have mercy on me, O God,
according to your steadfast love;
according to your abundant mercy
blot out my transgressions.
2Wash me thoroughly from my iniquity,
and cleanse me from my sin.
3For I know my transgressions ...

*Feeling
shame,
seeking help*

1 John 1:6-9

6If we say that we have fellowship with him
while we are walking in darkness,
we lie and do not do what is true;
7but if we walk in the light
as he himself is in the light,
we have fellowship with one another,
and the blood of Jesus his Son
cleanses us from all sin.
8If we say that we have no sin,
we deceive ourselves, and the truth is not in us.

*Self-
deception*

[9]If we confess our sins,
he who is faithful and just will forgive us our sins
and cleanse us from all unrighteousness.

Asking
forgiveness

Psalm 25:16-18
[16]Turn to me and be gracious to me,
for I am lonely and afflicted.
[17]Relieve the troubles of my heart,
and bring me out of my distress.
[18]Consider my affliction and my trouble,
and forgive all my sins.

Acknowledging
temptation

James 1:13-17
[13]No one, when tempted,
should say, 'I am being tempted by God';
for God cannot be tempted by evil
and he himself tempts no one.
[14]But one is tempted by one's own desire,
being lured and enticed by it;
[15]then, when that desire has conceived,
it gives birth to sin, and that sin,
when it is fully grown, gives birth to death.
[16]Do not be deceived, my beloved.
[17]Every generous act of giving,
with every perfect gift, is from above,
coming down from the Father of lights,
with whom there is no variation
or shadow due to change.

Forgiving

Luke 15:11-14, 15-20ff
[11]Then Jesus said,
'There was a man who had two sons.
[13]A few days later
the younger son gathered all he had
and travelled to a distant country.

14When he had spent everything,
a severe famine took place
throughout that country,
and he began to be in need …
18I will get up and go to my father,
and I will say to him,
'Father, I have sinned against heaven
and before you;
19I am no longer worthy to be called your son;
treat me like one of your hired hands.'
20So he set off and went to his father.
But while he was still far off,
his father saw him
and was filled with compassion;
he ran and put his arms around him and kissed him.

— God in the Busyness of Everyday —

John 4:7-10ff
7A Samaritan woman came to draw water,
and Jesus said to her,'Give me a drink.'
8(His disciples had gone to the city to buy food.)
9The Samaritan woman said to him,
'How is it that you, a Jew,
ask a drink of me, a woman of Samaria?'
(Jews do not share things in common with Samaritans.)
10Jesus answered her,
'If you knew the gift of God,
and who it is that is saying to you,
"Give me a drink",
you would have asked him,
and he would have given you living water …'

*Learning to
receive as
well as give*

Balancing   Hebrews 4:4
work and   For in one place
rest   it speaks about the seventh day as follows,
                'And God rested on the seventh day
                from all his works.'

Taking time Exodus 3:1-2, 5ff
out to notice [1]Moses was keeping the flock
                of his father-in-law Jethro, the priest of Midian
                he led his flock beyond the wilderness,
                and came to Horeb, the mountain of God.
                [2]There the angel of the Lord appeared to him
                in a flame of fire out of a bush;
                he looked, and the bush was blazing.
                [5]Then he said,'Come no closer!
                Remove the sandals from your feet,
                for the place on which you are standing is holy ground.'

Over-   Luke 12:23, 29
anxiety   [23]He said to his disciples,
about   'Therefore I tell you,
material   do not worry about your life,
survival   what you will eat, or about your body,
                For life is more than food,
                and the body more than clothing.
                [29]And do not keep striving
                for what you are to eat and
                what you are to drink,
                and do not keep worrying.

Prioritising Luke 10:38, 41-42ff
essentials   [38]Now as they went on their way,
                he entered a certain village,
                where a woman named Martha
                welcomed him into her home.

'Lord, do you not care that my sister
has left me to do all the work by myself?
Tell her then to help me.'
41But the Lord answered her,
'Martha, Martha, you are worried
and distracted by many things;
42there is need of only one thing.
Mary has chosen the better part,
which will not be taken away from her.'

1 Kings 19:11-12ff   *Finding a*
He said,'Go out and stand   *centre of*
on the mountain before the Lord,   *calm*
for the Lord is about to pass by.'
Now there was a great wind,
so strong that it was splitting mountains
and breaking rocks in pieces before the Lord,
but the Lord was not in the wind;
and after the wind an earthquake,
but the Lord was not in the earthquake;
12and after the earthquake a fire,
but the Lord was not in the fire;
and after the fire a sound of sheer silence.

Luke 12:16-18, 20-21ff   *When*
The land of a rich man produced abundantly.   *overdoing*
17And he thought to himself,   *the output*
'What should I do,
for I have no place to store my crops?'
18Then he said, 'I will do this:
I will pull down my barns and build larger ones.'
20But God said to him, 'You fool!
This very night your life is being demanded of you.
And the things you have prepared, whose will they be?'
21So it is with those who store up treasures
for themselves but are not rich toward God.

— *Grief and Loss* —

Needing comfort

John 20:11-16ff

11But Mary stood weeping
outside the tomb. As she wept,
she bent over to look into the tomb;
12and she saw two angels in white.
13They said to her,
'Woman, why are you weeping?'
She said to them,'They have taken away my Lord,
and I do not know where they have laid him.'
14When she had said this,
she turned around
and saw Jesus standing there,
16Jesus said to her,'Mary!'
She turned and said to him in Hebrew,
'Rabbouni!' (which means Teacher).

Is there life after death?

Romans 10: 8-9ff

8But what does it say?
'The word is near you,
on your lips and in your heart'
(that is, the word of faith that we proclaim);
9because if you confess with your lips
that Jesus is Lord
and believe in your heart
that God raised him from the dead,
you will be saved.

Struggling with loss

John 11:32, 38-40, 43ff

32When Mary came where Jesus was
and saw him, she knelt at his feet
and said to him,'Lord, if you had been here,
my brother would not have died.'
38Then Jesus, again greatly disturbed,
came to the tomb.

It was a cave, and a stone was lying against it.
[39]Jesus said,'Take away the stone.'
Martha, the sister of the dead man, said to him,
'Lord, already there is a stench
because he has been dead four days.'
[40]Jesus said to her,
'Did I not tell you that if you believed,
you would see the glory of God?'
[43]When he had said this, he cried with a loud voice,
'Lazarus, come out!'

Luke 23: 39-40a, 42-43ff   *Hearing the*
[39]One of the criminals   *promise of*
who were hanged there   *eternal life*
kept deriding him and saying,
'Are you not the Messiah?
Save yourself and us!'
[40]But the other rebuked him,
saying, 'Do you not fear God,
since you are under the same sentence
of condemnation?'
[42]Then he said,'Jesus, remember me
when you come into your kingdom.'
[43]He replied,'Truly I tell you,
today you will be with me in Paradise.'

Matthew 28:5-7ff   *Learning to*
[5]But the angel said to the women,   *look and*
'Do not be afraid;   *listen*
I know that you are looking for Jesus   *differently*
who was crucified.
[6]He is not here;
for he has been raised, as he said.
Come, see the place where he lay.
[7]Then go quickly and tell his disciples,

"He has been raised from the dead,
and indeed he is going ahead of you to Galilee;
there you will see him." This is my message for you.'

Fears
around
death

Revelation 22:1-6
[1]Then the angel showed me
the river of the water of life,
bright as crystal,
flowing from the throne of God and of the Lamb
[2]through the middle of the street of the city.
On either side of the river is the tree of life
with its twelve kinds of fruit,
producing its fruit each month;
and the leaves of the tree are for the healing of the nations.
[3]Nothing accursed will be found there any more.
But the throne of God and of the Lamb will be in it,
and his servants will worship him;
[4]they will see his face,
and his name will be on their foreheads.
[5]And there will be no more night;
they need no light of lamp or sun,
for the Lord God will be their light,
and they will reign forever and ever.
[6]And he said to me,
'These words are trustworthy and true,
for the Lord, the God of the spirits of the prophets,
has sent his angel to show his servants
what must soon take place.'

When I need
to weep

Revelation 21:1-4
[1]Then I saw a new heaven
and a new earth;
for the first heaven and the first earth
had passed away, and the sea was no more.
[2]And I saw the holy city, the new Jerusalem,
coming down out of heaven from God,

prepared as a bride adorned for her husband.
³And I heard a loud voice from the throne saying,
'See, the home of God is among mortals.
He will dwell with them as their God;
they will be his peoples,
and God himself will be with them;
⁴he will wipe every tear from their eyes.
Death will be no more; mourning and crying and pain
will be no more, for the first things have passed away.'

John 19:26-30   *Final*
Meanwhile, standing near the cross of Jesus   *moments*
were his mother, and his mother's sister,
Mary the wife of Cleopas, and Mary Magdalene.
²⁶When Jesus saw his mother
and the disciple whom he loved standing beside her,
he said to his mother,'Woman, here is your son.'
²⁷Then he said to the disciple,'Here is your mother.'
And from that hour
the disciple took her into his own home.
²⁸After this, when Jesus knew that all was now finished,
he said (in order to fulfil the scripture), 'I am thirsty.'
²⁹A jar full of sour wine was standing there.
So they put a sponge full of the wine
on a branch of hyssop and held it to his mouth.
³⁰When Jesus had received the wine, he said,
'It is finished.'
Then he bowed his head and gave up his spirit.

— Help —

Surrendering   2 Kings 5:11, 13-14
over-control   11But Naaman became angry
and went away, saying,
'I thought that for me
he would surely come out,
and stand and call on the name
of the Lord his God,
and would wave his hand over the spot,
and cure the leprosy!
13But his servants approached and said to him,
'Father, if the prophet had commanded you
to do something difficult, would you not have done it?
How much more, when all he said to you was,
"Wash, and be clean"?'
14So he went down and immersed himself seven times
in the Jordan, according to the word of the man of God;
his flesh was restored like the flesh of a young boy,
and he was clean.

Daring the   Mark 5:25, 27-28ff
first step to   25Now there was a woman
inner   who had been suffering from haemorrhages
healing   for twelve years.
27She had heard about Jesus,
and came up behind him in the crowd
and touched his cloak,
28for she said,'If I but touch his clothes,
I will be made well.'

Knowing   Mark 10:46b-51
what I need   Bartimaeus son of Timaeus,
to let go of   a blind beggar,
was sitting by the roadside.
47When he heard that it was Jesus of Nazareth,

he began to shout out and say,
'Jesus, Son of David, have mercy on me!'
[48]Many sternly ordered him to be quiet,
but he cried out even more loudly,
'Son of David, have mercy on me!'
[49]Jesus stood still and said, 'Call him here.'
And they called the blind man, saying to him,
'Take heart; get up, he is calling you.'
[50]So throwing off his cloak,
he sprang up and came to Jesus.
[51]Then Jesus said to him,
'What do you want me to do for you?'
The blind man said to him,
'My teacher, let me see again.'

Luke 5:12-13

When I need to hold on in trust

[12]Once, when he was in one of the cities,
there was a man covered with leprosy.
When he saw Jesus,
he bowed with his face to the ground
and begged him,
'Lord, if you choose,
you can make me clean.'
[13]Then Jesus stretched out his hand, touched him,
and said, 'I do choose. Be made clean.'
Immediately the leprosy left him.

Luke 8:41a-42, 49-50, 51-55

Coming back to myself

Just then there came a man named Jairus,
[42]for he had an only daughter,
about twelve years old, who was dying.
As he went, the crowds pressed in on him.
[49]While he was still speaking,
someone came from the leader's house to say,
'Your daughter is dead;
[53]And they laughed at him, knowing that she was dead.

[54]But he took her by the hand and called out,
'Child, get up!'
[55]Her spirit returned,
and she got up at once.

Asking help
for family
and
neighbours

Mk 1:30-32
[30]Now Simon's mother-in-law
was in bed with a fever,
and they told him about her at once.
[31]He came and took her by the hand
and lifted her up. Then the fever left her,
and she began to serve them.
[32]That evening, at sundown,
they brought to him all who were sick
or possessed with demons.

— *Indwelling Love* —

Remaining
conscious of
God's love

John 15:9
[9]As the Father has loved me,
so I have loved you; abide in my love.

Hearing
'I love you.'

Isaiah 43:1-3a, 4a
[1]But now thus says the Lord,
he who created you, O Jacob,
he who formed you, O Israel:
Do not fear, for I have redeemed you;
I have called you by name, you are mine.
[2]When you pass through the waters,
I will be with you;
and through the rivers,
they shall not overwhelm you;
when you walk through fire
you shall not be burned,
and the flame shall not consume you.
[3]For I am the Lord your God,

the Holy One of Israel,
your Saviour ...
⁴Because you are precious in my sight,
and honoured,
and I love you ...

Psalm 139:1-4, 9-10ff *Feeling*
¹O Lord, you have searched me *known and*
and known me. *loved*
²You know when I sit down
and when I rise up;
you discern my thoughts from far away.
³You search out my path and my lying down,
and are acquainted with all my ways.
⁴Even before a word is on my tongue,
O Lord, you know it completely.
⁹If I take the wings of the morning
and settle at the farthest limits of the sea,
¹⁰even there your hand shall lead me,
and your right hand shall hold me fast.

John 15:1-7 *Receiving*
¹'I am the true vine, *day-to-day*
and my Father is the vine-grower. *grace*
²He removes every branch in me that bears no fruit.
Every branch that bears fruit
he prunes to make it bear more fruit.
³You have already been cleansed
by the word that I have spoken to you.
⁴Abide in me as I abide in you.
Just as the branch cannot bear fruit by itself
unless it abides in the vine,
neither can you unless you abide in me.
⁵I am the vine, you are the branches.
Those who abide in me and I in them bear much fruit,
because apart from me you can do nothing.

⁶Whoever does not abide in me
is thrown away like a branch and withers;
such branches are gathered,
thrown into the fire, and burned.
⁷If you abide in me,
and my words abide in you,
ask for whatever you wish, and it will be done for you.

Knowing
where I
stand

1 John 3:1-2
¹See what love the Father has given us,
that we should be called children of God;
and that is what we are.
The reason the world does not know us
is that it did not know him.
²Beloved, we are God's children now;
what we will be has not yet been revealed.
What we do know is this:
when he is revealed, we will be like him,
for we will see him as he is.

God holding
my life, past
as well as
present

Hosea 11:1-4
¹When Israel was a child,
I loved him, and out of Egypt I called my son.
²The more I called them, the more they went from me;
³Yet it was I who taught Ephraim to walk,
I took them up in my arms;
but they did not know that I healed them.
⁴I led them with cords of human kindness,
with bands of love.
I was to them like those
who lift infants to their cheeks.
I bent down to them and fed them.

— *Leadership and responsibility* —

Exodus 4:10-12ff   *Entrusting*
[10]But Moses said to the Lord,   *my abilities*
'O my Lord, I have never been eloquent,
neither in the past nor even now
that you have spoken to your servant;
but I am slow of speech and slow of tongue.'
[11]Then the Lord said to him,
'Who gives speech to mortals?
Who makes them mute or deaf, seeing or blind?
Is it not I, the Lord?
[12]Now go, and I will be with your mouth
and teach you what you are to speak.'

Deuteronomy 1:17   *Freedom*
[17]You must not be partial in judging: *from human*
hear out the small and the great alike;   *respect*
you shall not be intimidated by anyone,
for the judgment is God's.
Any case that is too hard for you,
bring to me, and I will hear it.'

2 Cor 3:1-2   *Standing in*
[1]Therefore, since it is by God's mercy   *transparency*
that we are engaged in this ministry,
we do not lose heart.
[2]We have renounced the shameful things
that one hides; we refuse to practice cunning
or to falsify God's word;
but by the open statement of the truth
we commend ourselves
to the conscience of everyone
in the sight of God.

Acknowledg-   *Exodus 3:11-14*
ing a Power   [11]But Moses said to God,
greater than   'Who am I that I should go to Pharaoh,
one's own   and bring the Israelites out of Egypt?'
                   [12]He said,'I will be with you;
                   [13]But Moses said to God,
                   'If I come to the Israelites and say to them,
                   "The God of your ancestors
                   has sent me to you,"
                   and they ask me, "What is his name?"
                   what shall I say to them?'
                   [14]God said to Moses,
                   'I AM WHO I AM.'

Willingness   *Isaiah 6:1-8*
to go   [1]In the year that King Uzziah died,
forward   I saw the Lord sitting on a throne,
                   high and lofty;
                   and the hem of his robe filled the temple.
                   [2]Seraphs were in attendance above him …
                   [6]Then one of the seraphs flew to me,
                   holding a live coal that had been taken
                   from the altar with a pair of tongs.
                   [7]The seraph touched my mouth with it
                   and said: 'Now that this has touched your lips,
                   your guilt has departed and your sin is blotted out.'
                   [8]Then I heard the voice of the Lord saying,
                   'Whom shall I send, and who will go for us?'
                   And I said, 'Here am I; send me!'

Wanting   *Jeremiah 1: 5-6, 9*
courage   [5]'Before I formed you in the womb I knew you,
                   and before you were born I consecrated you;
                   I appointed you a prophet to the nations.'
                   [6]Then I said,'Ah, Lord God!
                   Truly I do not know how to speak, for I am only a boy.'

⁹Then the Lord put out his hand
and touched my mouth;
and the Lord said to me,
'Now I have put my words in your mouth.

John 2:2, 3, 6-7, 9ff   *Open to*
²On the third day there was a wedding   *transform-*
in Cana of Galilee   *ation*
³When the wine gave out,
the mother of Jesus said to him,
'They have no wine.'
⁶Now standing there were six stone water jars
for the Jewish rites of purification,
each holding twenty or thirty gallons.
⁷Jesus said to them,'Fill the jars with water.'
⁹When the steward tasted the water
that had become wine …

John 6:5, 8-9,11ff   *Offering the*
⁵When he looked up   *gifts I have*
and saw a large crowd coming toward him,
Jesus said to Philip,
'Where are we to buy bread for these people to eat?'
⁸One of his disciples, Andrew,
Simon Peter's brother, said to him,
⁹'There is a boy here
who has five barley loaves and two fish.
But what are they among so many people?'
¹¹Then Jesus took the loaves,
and when he had given thanks,
he distributed them to those
who were seated; so also the fish,
as much as they wanted.

When I need
to tell the
whole story   *Lk 24:13, 15, 17, 18b-19*

13Now on that same day
two of them were going to a village
called Emmaus, about seven miles from Jerusalem …
15Jesus himself came near and went with them …
17'What are you discussing with each other
while you walk along?'
They stood still, looking sad …
18b'Are you the only stranger in Jerusalem
who does not know the things
that have taken place there in these days?'

Discerning   19He asked them, 'What things?'
qualities for
a new role   *1 Kings 3:7-9*

7And now, O Lord my God,
you have made your servant king
in place of my father David,
although I am only a little child;
I do not know how to go out or come in.
8And your servant is in the midst of the people
whom you have chosen,
a great people, so numerous
they cannot be numbered or counted.
9Give your servant therefore
an understanding mind to govern your people,
able to discern between good and evil;
for who can govern this your great people?'

— *Living with Others* —

Galatians 6:1-5   *Mutual*
[1]My friends, if anyone   *support*
is detected in a transgression,
you who have received the Spirit
should restore such a one
in a spirit of gentleness.
Take care that you yourselves
are not tempted.
[2]Bear one another's burdens,
and in this way you will fulfill the law of Christ.
[4]All must test their own work;
then that work,
rather than their neighbour's work,
will become a cause for pride.
[5]For all must carry their own loads.

Philippians 4:5-8   *Nourishing*
[5]Let your gentleness   *inner and*
be known to everyone. The Lord is near.   *outer peace*
[6]Do not worry about anything,
but in everything by prayer
and supplication with thanksgiving
let your requests be made known to God.
[7]And the peace of God,
which surpasses all understanding,
will guard your hearts
and your minds in Christ Jesus.
[8]Finally, beloved, whatever is true,
whatever is honourable,
whatever is just, whatever is pure,
whatever is pleasing, whatever is commendable,
if there is any excellence
and if there is anything worthy of praise,
think about these things.

Struggling	*Luke 6:31-33, 35*
to widen my	[31]Do to others
heart	as you would have them do to you.
	[32]'If you love those who love you,
	what credit is that to you?
	For even sinners
	love those who love them.
	[33]If you do good
	to those who do good to you,
	what credit is that to you?
	For even sinners do the same.
	[35]But love your enemies,
	do good, and lend,
	expecting nothing in return.

Status	*Luke 22:24-26*
issues	[24]A dispute also arose among them
	as to which one of them
	was to be regarded as the greatest.
	[25]But he said to them,
	'The kings of the Gentiles lord it over them;
	and those in authority over them
	are called benefactors.
	[26]But not so with you;
	rather the greatest among you
	must become like the youngest,
	and the leader like one who serves.

When con-	*Col 3:12-15ff*
fronted by	[12]As God's chosen ones,
interpersonal	holy and beloved,
barriers	clothe yourselves with compassion,
	kindness, humility, meekness, and patience.
	[13]Bear with one another
	and, if anyone has a complaint against another,
	forgive each other;

just as the Lord has forgiven you,
so you also must forgive.
14Above all, clothe yourselves with love,
which binds everything together in perfect harmony.
15And let the peace of Christ rule in your hearts,
to which indeed you were called in the one body.
And be thankful.

Psalm 138:7-8   *Surviving*
7Though I walk   *ridicule*
in the midst of trouble,
you preserve me against the wrath
of my enemies;
you stretch out your hand,
and your right hand delivers me.
8The Lord will fulfil his purpose for me;
your steadfast love, O Lord, endures forever.
Do not forsake the work of your hands.

1 John 4:11-14   *Finding*
11Beloved, since God loved us so much,   *inspiration*
we also ought to love one another.   *for genuine*
12No one has ever seen God;   *love*
if we love one another, God lives in us,
and his love is perfected in us.
13By this we know that we abide in him
and he in us, because
he has given us of his Spirit.
14And we have seen and do testify
that the Father has sent his Son
as the Saviour of the world.

Acknowledg-
ing different
roles

Matthew 3:13-17

13Then Jesus came from Galilee
to John at the Jordan,
to be baptised by him.
14John would have prevented him,
saying,'I need to be baptised by you,
and do you come to me?'
15But Jesus answered him,
'Let it be so now;
for it is proper for us in this way
to fulfill all righteousness.'
Then he consented.
16And when Jesus had been baptised,
just as he came up from the water,
suddenly the heavens
were opened to him
and he saw the Spirit of God
descending like a dove
and alighting on him.
17And a voice from heaven said,
'This is my Son, the Beloved,
with whom am well pleased.'

Seeking a
basis for
mutual
respect

Romans 8:14-18

14For all who are led by the Spirit of God
are children of God.
15For you did not receive a spirit of slavery
to fall back into fear,
but you have received a spirit of adoption.
When we cry,'Abba! Father!'
16it is that very Spirit bearing witness
with our spirit that we are children of God,
17and if children, then heirs, heirs of God
and joint heirs with Christ – if, in fact, we suffer
with him so that we may also be glorified with him.
18I consider that the sufferings

of this present time
are not worth comparing with the glory
about to be revealed to us.

Galatians 2:22-26

Recognising the Spirit's gifts in my own life and others'

[22]By contrast, the fruit of the Spirit
is love, joy, peace, patience, kindness,
generosity, faithfulness,
[23]gentleness, and self-control.
There is no law against such things.
[24]And those who belong to Christ Jesus
have crucified the flesh
with its passions and desires.
[25]If we live by the Spirit,
let us also be guided by the Spirit.
[26]Let us not become conceited,
competing against one another,
envying one another.

Psalm 133

Grateful for harmony

[1]How very good and pleasant it is
when kindred live together in unity!
[2]It is like the precious oil on the head,
running down upon the beard,
on the beard of Aaron,
running down over the collar of his robes.
[3]It is like the dew of Hermon,
which falls on the mountains of Zion.
For there the Lord ordained his blessing,
life forevermore.

Inner   *John 10:27-30*
security   27My sheep hear my voice.
in my call   I know them, and they follow me.
                  28I give them eternal life,
                  and they will never perish.
                  No one will snatch them out of my hand.
                  29What my Father has given me
                  is greater than all else, and
                  no one can snatch it
                  out of the Father's hand.
                  30The Father and I are one.

Staying   Psalm 46:10
calmly   10'Be still, and know that I am God!
grounded

When   *1 John 4:18-21*
challenged   18There is no fear in love,
by love   but perfect love casts out fear;
                  for fear has to do with punishment,
                  and whoever fears
                  has not reached perfection in love.
                  19We love because he first loved us.
                  20Those who say,'I love God,'
                  and hate their brothers or sisters, are liars;
                  for those who do not love a brother or sister
                  whom they have seen, cannot love God
                  whom they have not seen.
                  21The commandment we have from him is this:
                  those who love God
                  must love their brothers and sisters also.

Deuteronomy 4: 29-31ff

*Just coping
… remem-
bering God's
promises*

[29]From there you will seek the Lord your God,
and you will find him if you search after him
with all your heart and soul.
[30]In your distress,
when all these things have happened to you
in time to come,
you will return to the Lord your God and heed him.
[31]Because the Lord your God is a merciful God,
he will neither abandon you nor destroy you;
he will not forget the covenant
with your ancestors that he swore to them.

Romans 12:6-12

*Delighting
in others'
particular
gifts*

[6]We have gifts that differ
according to the grace given to us:
prophecy, in proportion to faith;
[7]ministry, in ministering;
the teacher, in teaching;
[8]the exhorter, in exhortation;
the giver, in generosity;
the leader, in diligence;
the compassionate, in cheerfulness.
[9]Let love be genuine;
hate what is evil, hold fast to what is good;
[10]love one another with mutual affection;
outdo one another in showing honour.
[11]Do not lag in zeal,
be ardent in spirit, serve the Lord.
[12]Rejoice in hope,
be patient in suffering, persevere in prayer.

— Messengers of God —

Responding to God's invitation	Revelation 22:16-17

16It is I, Jesus,
who sent my angel to you
with this testimony for the churches.
I am the root and the descendant of David,
the bright morning star.
17The Spirit and the bride say, 'Come.'
And let everyone who hears say, 'Come.'
And let everyone who is thirsty come.
Let anyone who wishes
take the water of life as a gift.

Peace in discerning truth	Tobit 12:15-18ff

15'I am Raphael,
one of the seven angels who stand ready
and enter before the glory of the Lord.'
16The two of them were shaken;
they fell face down, for they were afraid.
17But he said to them, 'Do not be afraid;
peace be with you. Bless God forevermore.
18As for me, when I was with you,
I was not acting on my own will,
but by the will of God.
Bless him each and every day; sing his praises.

Remembering the inner child	Matthew 18:10

10Take care
that you do not despise
one of these little ones;
for, I tell you, in heaven
their angels continually see
the face of my Father in heaven.

Acts 12:7-9ff

⁷Suddenly an angel of the Lord
appeared and a light shone in the cell.
He tapped Peter on the side
and woke him, saying,'Get up quickly.'
And the chains fell off his wrists.
⁸The angel said to him,
'Fasten your belt and put on your sandals.'
He did so. Then he said to him,
'Wrap your cloak around you and follow me.'
⁹Peter went out and followed him;
he did not realise that what was happening
with the angel's help was real;
he thought he was seeing a vision.

When I need to be open and spontaneous in responding

Psalm 103:20

²⁰Bless the Lord, O you his angels,
you mighty ones who do his bidding,
obedient to his spoken word.
²¹Bless the Lord, all his hosts,
his ministers that do his will.
²²Bless the Lord, all his works,
in all places of his dominion.
Bless the Lord, O my soul.

Wanting to share praise with all creation

Psalm 91:1-4, 11-12

¹You who live in the shelter of the Most High,
who abide in the shadow of the Almighty,
²will say to the Lord,'My refuge and my fortress;
my God, in whom I trust.'
³For he will deliver you from the snare of the fowler
and from the deadly pestilence;
⁴he will cover you with his pinions,
and under his wings you will find refuge;
¹¹For he will command his angels concerning you
to guard you in all your ways.

Angel Guardians

¹²On their hands they will bear you up,
so that you will not dash your foot against a stone ...

Trusting   *Luke 1:18-19*
God's   ¹⁸Zechariah said to the angel,
messengers   'How will I know that this is so?
For I am an old man,
and my wife is getting on in years.'
¹⁹The angel replied,
'I am Gabriel. I stand in the presence of God,
and I have been sent to speak to you
and to bring you this good news.

— *Ministry* —

Accepting   2 Cor 4:7-10
limitation   ⁷But we have this treasure in clay jars,
so that it may be made clear
that this extraordinary power belongs to God
and does not come from us.
⁸We are afflicted in every way,
but not crushed; perplexed,
but not driven to despair;
⁹persecuted, but not forsaken;
struck down, but not destroyed;
¹⁰always carrying in the body
the death of Jesus, so that the life of Jesus
may also be made visible in our bodies.

Open to   Acts 3:2-6
being used   ²And a man lame from birth
by God   was being carried in.
People would lay him daily
at the gate of the temple called the Beautiful Gate
so that he could ask for alms
from those entering the temple.

3When he saw Peter and John
about to go into the temple, he asked them for alms.
4Peter looked intently at him, as did John,
and said,'Look at us.'
5And he fixed his attention on them,
expecting to receive something from them.
6But Peter said,'I have no silver or gold,
but what I have I give you;
in the name of Jesus Christ of Nazareth,
stand up and walk.'

Luke 6:20-23ff

Reassessing values

20Then he looked up at his disciples and said:
'Blessed are you who are poor,
for yours is the kingdom of God.
21Blessed are you who are hungry now,
for you will be filled.
Blessed are you who weep now, for you will laugh.
22Blessed are you when people hate you,
and when they exclude you, revile you,
and defame you on account of the Son of Man.
23Rejoice in that day and leap for joy,
for surely your reward is great in heaven;
for that is what their ancestors did to the prophets.

1 Thessalonians 5: 16-22ff

When routine loses freshness

16Rejoice always,
17pray without ceasing,
18give thanks in all circumstances;
for this is the will of God in Christ Jesus for you.
19Do not quench the Spirit.
20Do not despise the words of prophets,
21but test everything; hold fast to what is good;
22abstain from every form of evil.

Keeping   2 Peter 1:5-10
spiritual life   5For this very reason,
alive   you must make every effort
                   to support your faith with goodness,
                   and goodness with knowledge,
                   6and knowledge with self-control,
                   and self-control with endurance,
                   and endurance with godliness,
                   7and godliness with mutual affection,
                   and mutual affection with love.
                   8For if these things are yours
                   and are increasing among you,
                   they keep you from being ineffective
                   and unfruitful in the knowledge
                   of our Lord Jesus Christ.
                   10Therefore, brothers and sisters,
                   be all the more eager to confirm your call and election,
                   for if you do this, you will never stumble.

When   Luke 10:30-34ff
tempted to   30Jesus replied,
hold back   'A man was going down from Jerusalem to Jericho,
                   and fell into the hands of robbers, who stripped him,
                   beat him, and went away, leaving him half dead.
                   31Now by chance a priest was going down that road;
                   and when he saw him, he passed by on the other side.
                   32So likewise a Levite, when he came to the place
                   and saw him, passed by on the other side.
                   33But a Samaritan while travelling came near him;
                   and when he saw him, he was moved with pity.
                   34He went to him and bandaged his wounds,
                   having poured oil and wine on them.
                   Then he put him on his own animal,
                   brought him to an inn, and took care of him.

— *Needs met* —

Psalm 23   *In grateful*
[1]The Lord is my shepherd, I shall not want.   *content-*
[2]He makes me lie down in green pastures;   *ment*
he leads me beside still waters;
[3]he restores my soul.
He leads me in right paths
for his name's sake.
[5]You prepare a table before me
in the presence of my enemies;
you anoint my head with oil;
my cup overflows.
[6]Surely goodness and mercy shall follow me
all the days of my life,
and I shall dwell in the house of the Lord
my whole life long.

John 6:35-37   *When*
[35]Jesus said to them,   *experiencing*
'I am the bread of life.   *emptiness*
Whoever comes to me
will never be hungry,
and whoever believes in me
will never be thirsty.
[36]But I said to you
that you have seen me
and yet do not believe.
[37]Everything that
the Father gives me
will come to me,
and anyone who comes to me
I will never drive away;

Awareness   John 21:1, 3-7, 9ff
of being   [1]After these things Jesus showed himself again
waited for, to the disciples by the Sea of Tiberias;
fed   [3]Simon Peter said ... 'I am going fishing.'
              They said to him,'We will go with you.'
              They went out and got into the boat,
              but that night they caught nothing.
              [4]Just after daybreak, Jesus stood on the beach;
              but the disciples did not know that it was Jesus.
              [5]Jesus said to them,
              'Children, you have no fish, have you?'
              They answered him, 'No.'
              [6]He said to them,
              'Cast the net to the right side of the boat,
              and you will find some.'
              [7]That disciple whom Jesus loved said to Peter,
              'It is the Lord!'
              [9]When they had gone ashore,
              they saw a charcoal fire there, with fish on it, and bread.

Taking one Exodus 16:4, 15-17
day at a   [4]Then the Lord said to Moses,
time   'I am going to rain bread from heaven for you,
              and each day the people shall go out
              and gather enough for that day.
              [15]When the Israelites saw it,
              they said to one another,'What is it?'
              For they did not know what it was.
              Moses said to them,
              'It is the bread that the Lord has given you to eat.
              [16]This is what the Lord has commanded:
              "Gather as much of it as each of you needs,
              an omer to a person according to the number of persons,
              all providing for those in their own tents".'
              [17]The Israelites did so, some gathering more, some less.

1 Kings 19:4-7   *When*
⁴But he himself went a day's journey   *resources*
into the wilderness,   *have run*
and came and sat down under a solitary broom tree.   *out*
He asked that he might die:
'It is enough; now, O Lord, take away my life,
for I am no better than my ancestors.'
⁵Then he lay down under the broom tree
and fell asleep. Suddenly an angel touched him
and said to him,'Get up and eat.'
⁶He looked, and there at his head
was a cake baked on hot stones, and a jar of water.
He ate and drank, and lay down again.
⁷The angel of the Lord came a second time,
touched him, and said,'Get up and eat,
otherwise the journey will be too much for you.'

— *Prayer* —

Philippians 4:6   *Asking with*
⁶Do not worry about anything,   *thanks*
but in everything by prayer
and supplication with thanksgiving
let your requests be made known to God.

Luke 6:12   *Praying in*
¹²Now during those days   *the darkness*
he went out to the mountain to pray;
and he spent the night in prayer to God.

Luke 11:1-2ff   *What to*
¹He was praying in a certain place,   *say?*
and after he had finished,
one of his disciples said to him,
'Lord, teach us to pray,
as John taught his disciples.'…

²He said to them,'When you pray, say:
Father, hallowed be your name …

Staying	*Luke 11:5, 8-9ff*
with prayer	⁵And he said to them,

⁵And he said to them,
'Suppose one of you has a friend,
and you go to him at midnight
and say to him, "Friend, lend me three loaves of bread …"
⁸I tell you, even though he will not get up
and give him anything because he is his friend,
at least because of his persistence
he will get up and give him whatever he needs.
⁹So I say to you, ask, and it will be given you
search, and you will find;
knock, and the door will be opened for you.

Preparing to   *Ezekiel 3:22-23ff*
really listen   ²²Then the hand of the Lord
was upon me there;
and he said to me,
Rise up, go out into the valley,
and there I will speak with you.
²³So I rose up and went out into the valley;
and the glory of the Lord stood there,
like the glory that I had seen by the river Chebar;
and I fell on my face.

Inclusive   1 Timothy 2:1-4
prayer   ¹First of all, then, I urge that supplications,
prayers, intercessions, and thanksgivings
be made for everyone,
²for kings and all who are in high positions,
so that we may lead a quiet and peaceable life
in all godliness and dignity.
³This is right and is acceptable
in the sight of God our Saviour,

⁴who desires everyone to be saved
 and to come to the knowledge of the truth.

Matthew 18:19-20   *Praying*
¹⁹Again, truly I tell you,   *together*
if two of you agree on earth
about anything you ask,
it will be done for you
by my Father in heaven.
²⁰For where two or three
are gathered in my name,
I am there among them.

— *Reassurance* —

Psalm 119:105   *Centring*
¹⁰⁵Your word   *the heart*
is a lamp to my feet
and a light to my path.

Exodus 13:21-22   *When in*
²¹The Lord went in front of them   *need of*
in a pillar of cloud by day,   *guidance*
to lead them along the way,
and in a pillar of fire by night,
to give them light,
so that they might travel
by day and by night.
²²Neither the pillar of cloud by day
nor the pillar of fire by night
left its place in front of the people.

When particularly vulnerable	*Deuteronomy 32:10-13*

¹⁰He sustained him in a desert land,
in a howling wilderness waste;
he shielded him, cared for him,
guarded him as the apple of his eye.
¹¹As an eagle stirs up its nest,
and hovers over its young; as it spreads its wings,
takes them up, and bears them aloft on its pinions,
¹²the Lord alone guided him;
no foreign god was with him.
¹³He set him atop the heights of the land,
and fed him with produce of the field;
he nursed him with honey from the crags,
with oil from flinty rock;

When I feel I'm sinking   *Matthew 14:23, 29-31ff*

²³Peter answered him,
'Lord, if it is you,
command me to come to you on the water.'
²⁹He said, 'Come.'
So Peter got out of the boat,
started walking on the water, and came toward Jesus.
³⁰But when he noticed the strong wind,
he became frightened, and beginning to sink,
he cried out, 'Lord, save me!'
³¹Jesus immediately reached out his hand
and caught him, saying to him,
'You of little faith, why did you doubt?'

When things don't make sense any more   *Jeremiah 18:2-6*

²'Come, go down to the potter's house,
and there I will let you hear my words.'
³So I went down to the potter's house,
and there he was working at his wheel.
⁴The vessel he was making of clay
was spoiled in the potter's hand,

and he reworked it into another vessel,
as seemed good to him.
⁵Then the word of the Lord came to me:
⁶Can I not do with you, O house of Israel,
just as this potter has done? says the Lord.
Just like the clay in the potter's hand,
so are you in my hand, O house of Israel.

Luke 9:28-31, 33-35

*Getting
the bigger
picture*

²⁸Now about eight days after these sayings
Jesus took with him Peter and John and James,
and went up on the mountain to pray.
²⁹And while he was praying,
the appearance of his face changed,
and his clothes became dazzling white.
³⁰Suddenly they saw two men,
Moses and Elijah, talking to him.
³¹They appeared in glory
and were speaking of his departure,
which he was about to accomplish at Jerusalem.
³³Just as they were leaving him,
Peter said to Jesus,
'Master, it is good for us to be here;
let us make three dwellings,
one for you, one for Moses, and one for Elijah' …
³⁴While he was saying this,
a cloud came an overshadowed them;
and they were terrified as they entered the cloud.
³⁵Then from the cloud came a voice that said,
'This is my Son, my Chosen; listen to him!'

Suffering   *1 Peter 1:3-7*

3Blessed be the God and Father
of our Lord Jesus Christ!
By his great mercy
he has given us a new birth
into a living hope
through the resurrection of Jesus Christ from the dead,
4and into an inheritance that is imperishable,
undefiled, and unfading, kept in heaven for you,
5who are being protected by the power of God
through faith for a salvation ready to be revealed
in the last time.
6In this you rejoice,
even if now for a little while
you have had to suffer various trials,
7so that the genuineness of your faith –
being more precious than gold that,
though perishable, is tested by fire –
may be found to result in praise and glory and honour
when Jesus Christ is revealed.

Confusion   *Luke 24:36-41*

36While they were talking about this,
Jesus himself stood among them
and said to them,'Peace be with you.'
37They were startled and terrified,
and thought that they were seeing a ghost.
38He said to them,
'Why are you frightened,
and why do doubts arise in your hearts?
39Look at my hands and my feet;
see that it is I myself. Touch me and see;
for a ghost does not have flesh and bones
as you see that I have.'
40And when he had said this,
he showed them his hands and his feet.

41While in their joy they were disbelieving
and still wondering, he said to them,
'Have you anything here to eat?'

John 6:16-21   *When*
16When evening came,   *battling on*
his disciples went down to the sea,   *alone*
17got into a boat,
and started across the sea to Capernaum.
It was now dark, and Jesus had not yet come to them.
18The sea became rough
because a strong wind was blowing.
19When they had rowed about three or four miles,
they saw Jesus walking on the sea
and coming near the boat, and they were terrified.
20But he said to them, 'It is I; do not be afraid.'
21Then they wanted to take him into the boat,
and immediately the boat
reached the land toward which they were going.

Psalm 16:1-2, 7-11   *When*
1Protect me, O God, for in you I take refuge.   *needing help*
2I say to the Lord, 'You are my Lord;   *with sexual*
I have no good apart from you.'   *problems*
7I bless the Lord who gives me counsel;   *and body*
in the night also my heart instructs me.   *issues*
8I keep the Lord always before me;
because he is at my right hand, I shall not be moved.
9Therefore my heart is glad,
and my soul rejoices;
my body also rests secure.
10For you do not give me up to Sheol,
or let your faithful one see the Pit.
11You show me the path of life.
In your presence there is fullness of joy;
in your right hand are pleasures forevermore.

— *Self-care* —

Weighing up values	Romans 12:2ff [2]Do not be conformed to this world, but be transformed by the renewing of your minds, so that you may discern what is the will of God, what is good and acceptable and perfect.
Taking quiet time alone	Mark 6:46-47 [46]After saying farewell to them, he went up on the mountain to pray. [47]When evening came, the boat was out on the sea, and he was alone on the land.
Becoming stale	Luke 14:34-35 Salt is good; but if salt has lost its taste, how can its saltiness be restored? [35]It is fit neither for the soil nor for the manure pile; they throw it away. Let anyone with ears to hear listen!'
Responsibility in sexual and social behaviour	1 Cor 6:19-20 [19]Do you not know that your body is a temple of the Holy Spirit within you, which you have from God? You are not your own; [20]you were bought with a price. So glorify God in your body.

Exodus 16:29-30   *Honouring*
²⁹See! The Lord has given you the sabbath,   *Sabbath rest*
therefore on the sixth day
he gives you food for two days;
each of you stay where you are;
do not leave your place on the seventh day.'
³⁰So the people rested on the seventh day.

Philippians 4:8   *When there*
⁸Finally, beloved, whatever is true,   *is too much*
whatever is honourable,   *going on*
whatever is just, whatever is pure,
whatever is pleasing, whatever is commendable,
if there is any excellence
and if there is anything worthy of praise,
think about these things.

— *Self-esteem* —

Psalm 17:8   *God's*
⁸Guard me as the apple of the eye;   *handiwork*
hide me in the shadow of your wings,

Luke 12:6-7   *Reflecting*
⁶Are not five sparrows   *on my*
sold for two pennies?   *uniqueness*
Yet not one of them
is forgotten in God's sight.
⁷But even the hairs of your head
are all counted.
Do not be afraid;
you are of more value than many sparrows.

When feeling 'useless'	**Luke 4:5-6a, 8, 11**

⁵Simon answered,
'Master, we have worked
all night long but have caught nothing.
Yet if you say so, I will let down the nets.'
⁶When they had done this,
they caught so many fish
that their nets were beginning to break.
And they came and filled both boats,
so that they began to sink.
⁸But when Simon Peter saw it,
he fell down at Jesus' knees, saying,
'Go away from me, Lord, for I am a sinful man!'
Then Jesus said to Simon,
'Do not be afraid;
from now on you will be catching people.'

Older-age gifts

Psalm 92:12-15

¹²The righteous flourish like the palm tree,
and grow like a cedar in Lebanon.
¹³They are planted in the house of the Lord;
they flourish in the courts of our God.
¹⁴In old age they still produce fruit;
they are always green and full of sap,
¹⁵showing that the Lord is upright;
he is my rock, and there is no unrighteousness in him.

Acknowledg-ing inner beauty

2 Cor 3:17-18

¹⁷Now the Lord is the Spirit,
and where the Spirit of the Lord is,
there is freedom.
¹⁸And all of us, with unveiled faces,
seeing the glory of the Lord
as though reflected in a mirror,
are being transformed
into the same image

from one degree of glory
to another; for this comes
from the Lord, the Spirit.

Ephesians 3:16-20   *Receiving*
[16]I pray that,   *strength*
according to the riches of his glory,
he may grant
that you may be strengthened in your inner being
with power through his Spirit,
[17]and that Christ
may dwell in your hearts through faith,
as you are being rooted and grounded in love.
[18]I pray that you may have the power to comprehend,
with all the saints,
what is the breadth and length and height and depth,
[19]and to know the love of Christ
that surpasses knowledge,
so that you may be filled with all the fullness of God.
[20]Now to him who by the power at work within us
is able to accomplish abundantly
far more than all we can ask or imagine.

Ephesians 1:7, 18-19   *Hope-filled*
[7]I pray   *possibilities*
that the God of our Lord Jesus Christ,
the Father of glory,
may give you a spirit
of wisdom and revelation
as you come to know him,
[18]so that, with the eyes of your heart enlightened,
you may know what is the hope
to which he has called you,
what are the riches
of his glorious inheritance
among the saints,

19and what is the immeasurable greatness
of his power for us who believe,
according to the working of his great power.

Struggling   1 Corinthians 12:4-11
with   4Now there are varieties of gifts,
jealousy/   but the same Spirit;
envy   5and there are varieties of service,
                 but the same Lord;
                 6and there are varieties of working,
                 but it is the same God
                 who inspires them all in every one.
                 7To each is given the manifestation of the Spirit
                 for the common good.
                 8To one is given through the Spirit
                 the utterance of wisdom,
                 and to another the utterance of knowledge
                 according to the same Spirit,
                 9to another faith by the same Spirit,
                 to another gifts of healing by the one Spirit,
                 10to another the working of miracles,
                 to another prophecy,
                 to another the ability to distinguish between spirits,
                 to another various kinds of tongues,
                 to another the interpretation of tongues.
                 11All these are inspired by one and the same Spirit,
                 who apportions to each one individually as he wills.

Appreciating   Mark 12:41-44
the richness   41He sat down opposite the treasury,
of   and watched the crowd putting money
authenticity   into the treasury.
                 Many rich people put in large sums.
                 42A poor widow came
                 and put in two small copper coins,
                 which are worth a penny.

43Then he called his disciples and said to them,
'Truly I tell you,
this poor widow has put in more
than all those who are contributing to the treasury.
44For all of them have contributed out of their abundance;
but she out of her poverty
has put in everything she had, all she had to live on.'

Psalm 139:13-18   *Nothing*
13For it was you who formed my inward parts;   *to hide*
you knit me together in my mother's womb.
14I praise you, for I am fearfully and wonderfully made.
Wonderful are your works;
that I know very well.
15My frame was not hidden from you,
when I was being made in secret,
intricately woven in the depths of the earth.
16Your eyes beheld my unformed substance.
In your book were written
all the days that were formed for me,
when none of them as yet existed.
17How weighty to me are your thoughts, O God!
How vast is the sum of them!
18I try to count them – they are more than the sand;
I come to the end – I am still with you.

— *Social Commitment* —

Micah 6:8   *Setting a*
8He has told you, O mortal, what is good;   *personal*
and what does the Lord require of you   *standard*
but to do justice, and to love kindness,
 and to walk humbly with your God?

Hearing the   Luke 1:46-55
call to do
justice

46And Mary said,'My soul magnifies the Lord,

47and my spirit rejoices in God my Savior,

48for he has looked with favour
on the lowliness of his servant.
Surely, from now on all generations
will call me blessed;

49for the Mighty One
has done great things for me,
and holy is his name.

50His mercy is for those who fear him
from generation to generation.

51He has shown strength with his arm;
he has scattered the proud
in the thoughts of their hearts.

52He has brought down the powerful
from their thrones, and lifted up the lowly;

53he has filled the hungry with good things,
and sent the rich away empty.

54He has helped his servant Israel,
in remembrance of his mercy,

55according to the promise
he made to our ancestors,
to Abraham and to his descendants forever.'

When called   Luke 3:2b-4
to go it
alone

2bThe word of God came to John
son of Zechariah in the wilderness.

3He went into all the region around the Jordan,
proclaiming a baptism of repentance
for the forgiveness of sins,

4as it is written in the book of the words
of the prophet Isaiah,
'The voice of one crying out in the wilderness:
"Prepare the way of the Lord, make his paths straight".'

Lk 5:18-20, 24

*Reluctance
to offer/
accept new
approaches*

18Just then some men came,
carrying a paralysed man on a bed.
They were trying to bring him in
and lay him before Jesus;
19but finding no way to bring him in
because of the crowd,
they went up on the roof
and let him down with his bed
through the tiles
into the middle of the crowd in front of Jesus.
20When he saw their faith, he said,
'Friend, your sins are forgiven you.'
24But so that you may know that the Son of Man
has authority on earth to forgive sins'
And he said to the one who was paralysed,
'I say to you, stand up and take your bed
and go to your home.'

John 14:12-14

*When
doubting
the out-
come*

12Very truly, I tell you,
the one who believes in me
will also do the works that I do and,
in fact, will do greater works
than these, because I am going to the Father.
13I will do whatever you ask in my name,
so that the Father may be glorified in the Son.
14If in my name you ask me for anything, I will do it.

Luke 6:36-37

Equality

36Be merciful,
just as your Father is merciful.
37Do not judge, and you will not be judged;
do not condemn,
and you will not be condemned.
Forgive, and you will be forgiven.

Speaking   *Luke 21:10-13ff*
from the   10Then he aid to them,
cutting edge 'Nation will rise against nation,
and kingdom against kingdom;
11there will be great earthquakes,
and in various places famines and plagues;
and there will be dreadful portents
and great signs from heaven.
12But before all this occurs,
they will arrest you and persecute you;
they will hand you over to synagogues and prisons,
and you will be brought before kings
and governors because of my name.
13This will give you an opportunity to testify.

Facing up to *Romans 8:14-18*
bureaucratic 14For all who are led
obstacles   by the Spirit of God are children of God.
15For you did not receive a spirit of slavery
to fall back into fear,
but you have received a spirit of adoption.
When we cry, 'Abba! Father!'
16it is that very Spirit bearing witness
with our spirit that we are children of God,
17and if children, then heirs, heirs of God
and joint heirs with Christ
– if, in fact, we suffer with him
– so that we may also be glorified with him.
18I consider that the sufferings
of this present time
are not worth comparing
with the glory about to be revealed to us.

Romans 10:12
[12]For there is no distinction
between Jew and Greek;
the same Lord is Lord of all
and is generous to all who call on him.

— *Starting Again* —

Matthew 9:10-13
[10]And as he sat at dinner in the house,
many tax collectors and sinners came
and were sitting with him and his disciples.
[11]When the Pharisees saw this,
they said to his disciples,
'Why does your teacher
eat with tax collectors and sinners?'
[12]But when he heard this, he said,
'Those who are well
have no need of a physician,
but those who are sick.
[13]Go and learn what this means,
"I desire mercy, not sacrifice."
For I have come to call
not the righteous but sinners.'

Luke 13:34
[34]Jerusalem, Jerusalem,
the city that kills the prophets
and stones those who are sent to it!
How often have I desired
to gather your children together
as a hen gathers her brood
under her wings,
and you were not willing!

Time to
make
amends

Luke 19:1-6, 8ff

[1]He entered Jericho
and was passing through it.
[2]A man was there named Zacchaeus;
he was a chief tax collector and was rich.
[3]He was trying to see who Jesus was,
but on account of the crowd he could not,
because he was short in stature.
[4]So he ran ahead
and climbed a sycamore tree to see him,
because he was going to pass that way.
[5]When Jesus came to the place,
he looked up and said to him,
'Zacchaeus, hurry and come down;
for I must stay at your house today.'
[6]So he hurried down and was happy to welcome him.
[8]Zacchaeus stood there and said to the Lord,
'Look, half of my possessions, Lord,
I will give to the poor;
and if I have defrauded anyone of anything,
I will pay back four times as much.'

Time to take
a new path

1 John 4:9-10

[9]God's love
was revealed among us in this way:
God sent his only Son
into the world
so that we might live through him.
[10]In this is love,
not that we loved God
but that he loved us and sent his Son
to be the atoning sacrifice for our sins.

Psalm 9:9-10

⁹The Lord
is a stronghold for the oppressed,
a stronghold in times of trouble.
¹⁰And those who know your name
put their trust in you,
for you, O Lord,
have not forsaken those who seek you.

Knowing
God's name
from
personal
experience

Romans 6:3-4ff

³Do you not know
that all of us
who have been baptised
into Christ Jesus
were baptised into his death?
⁴Therefore we have been buried
with him by baptism into death,
so that, just as Christ was raised from the dead
by the glory of the Father,
so we too might walk in newness of life.

Worth the
effort?

Galatians 4:4-7

⁴But when the fullness of time had come,
God sent his Son, born of a woman,
born under the law,
⁵in order to redeem those
who were under the law,
so that we might receive adoption as children.
⁶And because you are children,
God has sent the Spirit of his Son
into our hearts, crying,'Abba! Father!'
⁷So you are no longer a slave
but a child, and if a child
then also an heir, through God.

Claiming
my real
spiritual
home

Feeling
welcomed
and wanted

Luke 15:4-7

4Which one of you,
having a hundred sheep
and losing one of them,
does not leave the ninety-nine
in the wilderness and go after the one
that is lost until he finds it?
5When he has found it,
he lays it on his shoulders and rejoices.
6And when he comes home,
he calls together his friends and neighbours,
saying to them, 'Rejoice with me,
for I have found my sheep that was lost.'
7Just so, I tell you, there will be more joy in heaven
over one sinner who repents
than over ninety-nine righteous persons
who need no repentance.

— *Stuck* —

Excuses

John 5:2-8ff

2Now in Jerusalem by the Sheep Gate
there is a pool, called in Hebrew Beth-zatha,
which has five porticoes.
3In these lay many invalids
– blind, lame, and paralysed.
5One man was there
who had been ill for thirty-eight years.
6When Jesus saw him lying there
and knew that he had been there a long time,
he said to him,'Do you want to be made well?'
7The sick man answered him,
'Sir, I have no one to put me into the pool
when the water is stirred up;
and while I am making my way,
someone else steps down ahead of me.'
8Jesus said to him,'Stand up, take your mat and walk.'

Mark 7:32-35ff

³²They brought to him a deaf man
who had an impediment in his speech;
and they begged him to lay his hand on him.
³³He took him aside in private, away from the crowd,
and put his fingers into his ears,
and he spat and touched his tongue.
³⁴Then looking up to heaven,
he sighed and said to him,'Ephphatha,'
that is,'Be opened.'
³⁵And immediately his ears were opened,
his tongue was released, and he spoke plainly.

Closing my ears

Luke 13: 11-12

¹¹And just then there appeared a woman
with a spirit that had crippled her
for eighteen years.
She was bent over
and was quite unable to stand up straight.
¹²When Jesus saw her,
he called her over and said,
'Woman, you are set free from your ailment.'

Needing to name the baggage

Matthew 25: 2-4, 8-10ff

Ten bridesmaids took their lamps
and went to meet the bridegroom.
²Five of them were foolish,
and five were wise.
³When the foolish took their lamps,
they took no oil with them;
⁴but the wise took flasks of oil with their lamps.
⁸The foolish said to the wise,
'Give us some of your oil, for our lamps are going out.'
⁹But the wise replied,
'No! there will not be enough for you
and for us;

Avoiding responsibility

you had better go to the dealers
and buy some for yourselves.'
10And while they went to buy it,
the bridegroom came, and those who were ready
went with him into the wedding banquet;
and the door was shut.

Struggling John 20:24-27
with belief 24But Thomas (who was called the Twin),
one of the twelve, was not with them when Jesus came.
25So the other disciples told him,
'We have seen the Lord.'
But he said to them,
'Unless I see the mark
of the nails in his hands,
and put my finger in the mark of the nails
and my hand in his side, I will not believe.'
Although the doors were shut,
Jesus came and stood among them
and said,'Peace be with you.'
27Then he said to Thomas,
'Put your finger here and see my hands.
Reach out your hand and put it in my side.
Do not doubt but believe.'

Resistance Mark 3:4-8
4Listen! A sower went out to sow
And as he sowed,
some seed fell on the path,
and the birds came and ate it up.
5Other seed fell on rocky ground,
where it did not have much soil,
and it sprang up quickly,
since it had no depth of soil.
6And when the sun rose,
it was scorched;

and since it had no root,
it withered away.
⁷Other seed fell among thorns
and the thorns grew up and choked it,
and it yielded no grain.
⁸Other seed fell into good soil ...

Luke 12:55b-56   *Looking the*
When you see a cloud rising in the west,   *other way*
you immediately say, 'It is going to rain';
and so it happens.
And when you see the south wind blowing,
you say, 'There will be scorching heat';
and it happens.
⁵⁶ You hypocrites!
You know how to interpret
the appearance of earth and sky,
but why do you not know
how to interpret the present time?

Luke 14:16-20ff   *Good*
Then Jesus said to him,   *intentions,*
'Someone gave a great dinner and invited many.   *but ...*
¹⁷At the time for the dinner he sent his slave
to say to those who had been invited,
"Come; for everything is ready now."
¹⁸But they all alike began to make excuses.
The first said to him,
"I have bought a piece of land,
and I must go out and see it;
please accept my regrets."
¹⁹Another said, "I have bought five yoke of oxen,
and I am going to try them out; please accept my regrets."
²⁰Another said, "I have just been married,
and therefore I cannot come." ...

— *Thanksgiving* —

Looking
back with
gratitude

Psalm 107:1-7ff

1O give thanks to the Lord, for he is good;
for his steadfast love endures forever.
2Let the redeemed of the Lord say so,
those he redeemed from trouble
3and gathered in from the lands,
from the east and from the west,
from the north and from the south.
4Some wandered in desert wastes,
finding no way to an inhabited town;
5hungry and thirsty,
their soul fainted within them.
6Then they cried to the Lord in their trouble,
and he delivered them from their distress;
7he led them by a straight way,

Relief
and joy

Psalm 18:1-3, 31-32

1I love you, O Lord, my strength.
2The Lord is my rock,
my fortress, and my deliverer,
my God, my rock in whom I take refuge,
my shield, and the horn of my salvation,
my stronghold.
3I call upon the Lord,
who is worthy to be praised,
so I shall be saved from my enemies.
31For who is God except the Lord?
And who is a rock besides our God? –
32the God who girded me with strength,
and made my way safe.

Luke 2:27-32

27Guided by the Spirit,
Simeon came into the temple;
and when the parents
brought in the child Jesus,
to do for him what was customary under the law
28Simeon took him in his arms
and praised God, saying,
29'Master, now you are
dismissing your servant
in peace, according to your word;
30for my eyes have seen your salvation,
31which you have prepared
in the presence of all peoples,
32a light for revelation to the Gentiles
and for glory to your people Israel.'

Psalm 131

O Lord, my heart is not lifted up,
my eyes are not raised too high;
I do not occupy myself with things
too great and too marvellous for me.
2But I have calmed and quieted my soul,
like a weaned child with its mother;
my soul is like the weaned child that is with me.
3O Israel, hope in the Lord
from this time on and forevermore.

Psalm 89:1-4

1I will sing of your steadfast love,
O Lord, forever;
with my mouth I will proclaim your faithfulness
to all generations.
2I declare that your steadfast love is established forever;
your faithfulness is as firm as the heavens.

3You said,'I have made a covenant with my chosen one,
I have sworn to my servant David:
4"I will establish your descendants forever,
and build your throne for all generations".'

Feeling part
of the whole

1 Chronicles 10:10-13
10Then David blessed the Lord
in the presence of all the assembly;
David said:'Blessed are you, O Lord,
the God of our ancestor Israel,
forever and ever.
11Yours, O Lord, are the greatness,
the power, the glory, the victory,
and the majesty;
for all that is in the heavens
and on the earth is yours;
yours is the kingdom, O Lord,
and you are exalted as head above all.
12Riches and honour come from you,
and you rule over all.
In your hand are power and might;
and it is in your hand to make great
and to give strength to all.
13And now, our God,
we give thanks to you and praise your glorious name …

Remembering
blessings

Ephesians 1:3-12
3Blessed be the God and Father
of our Lord Jesus Christ,
who has blessed us in Christ
with every spiritual blessing in the heavenly places,
4just as he chose us in Christ
before the foundation of the world
to be holy and blameless before him in love.
5He destined us for adoption as his children
through Jesus Christ,

according to the good pleasure of his will,
6to the praise of his glorious grace
that he freely bestowed on us in the Beloved.
7In him we have redemption through his blood,
the forgiveness of our trespasses,
according to the riches of his grace
8that he lavished on us.

Philippians 4: 4-7   *Whole-*
4Rejoice in the Lord always;   *hearted*
again I will say, Rejoice.   *delight in*
5Let your gentleness   *life's gifts*
be known to everyone.
The Lord is near.
6Do not worry about anything,
but in everything by prayer and supplication
with thanksgiving
let your requests be made known to God.
7And the peace of God,
which surpasses all understanding,
will guard your hearts and your minds in Christ Jesus.

— *Waiting* —

Isaiah 40:28-31   *When*
28Have you not known?   *energy is*
Have you not heard?   *running out*
The Lord is the everlasting God,
the Creator of the ends of the earth.
He does not faint or grow weary;
his understanding is unsearchable.
29He gives power to the faint,
and strengthens the powerless.
30Even youths will faint and be weary,
and the young will fall exhausted;

31but those who wait for the Lord
shall renew their strength,
they shall mount up with wings like eagles,
they shall run and not be weary
they shall walk and not faint.

Longing for   *Psalm 42:1-5ff*
spiritual   1As a deer longs for flowing streams,
intimacy   so my soul longs for you, O God.
2My soul thirsts for God,
for the living God.
When shall I come
and behold the face of God?
3My tears have been my food day and night,
while people say to me continually,
'Where is your God?'
5Why are you cast down, O my soul,
and why are you disquieted within me?
Hope in God; for I shall again praise him,
my help and my God.

When   *John 14:1-14*
feeling   1'Do not let your hearts be troubled.
displaced   Believe in God, believe also in me.
2In my Father's house
there are many dwelling places.
If it were not so, would I have told you
that I go to prepare a place for you?
3And if I go and prepare a place for you,
I will come again and will take you to myself,
so that where I am, there you may be also.
4And you know the way
to the place where I am going.'
5Thomas said to him,
'Lord, we do not know where you are going.
How can we know the way?'

Psalm 13 *Enduring*

¹How long, O Lord? Will you forget me forever?
How long will you hide your face from me?
²How long must I bear pain in my soul,
and have sorrow in my heart all day long?
How long shall my enemy be exalted over me?
³Consider and answer me, O Lord my God!
Give light to my eyes, or I will sleep the sleep of death,
⁴and my enemy will say,'I have prevailed';
my foes will rejoice because I am shaken.
⁵But I trusted in your steadfast love;
my heart shall rejoice in your salvation.
⁶I will sing to the Lord,
because he has dealt bountifully with me.

Luke 2:8-11 *Staying
alert
in hope*

⁸In that region there were shepherds
living in the fields, keeping watch
over their flock by night.
⁹Then an angel of the Lord stood before them,
and the glory of the Lord shone around them,
and they were terrified.
¹⁰But the angel said to them, 'Do not be afraid;
for see – I am bringing you good news of great joy
for all the people:
¹¹to you is born this day in the city of David a Saviour,
who is the Messiah, the Lord.

Genesis 7:18-19, 8:10-13 *Taking
initiative*

¹⁸The flood continued forty days on the earth;
and the waters increased, and bore up the ark,
and it rose high above the earth.
¹⁹The waters swelled so mightily on the earth
that all the high mountains
under the whole heaven were covered;
And God made a wind blow over the earth,

and the waters subsided;
8:10He waited another seven days,
and again he sent out the dove from the ark;
11and the dove came back to him in the evening,
and there in its beak was a freshly plucked olive leaf;
so Noah knew that the waters
had subsided from the earth.
12Then he waited another seven days,
and sent out the dove;
and it did not return to him any more.
13In the six hundred first year, in the first month,
the first day of the month,
the waters were dried up from the earth;
and Noah removed the covering of the ark,
and looked, and saw
that the face of the ground was drying.

Hanging on   *Psalm 25*
1To you, O Lord, I lift up my soul.
2O my God, in you I trust;
do not let me be put to shame;
do not let my enemies exult over me.
3Do not let those who wait for you
be put to shame;
let them be ashamed
who are wantonly treacherous.
4Make me to know your ways, O Lord;
teach me your paths.
5Lead me in your truth, and teach me,
for you are the God of my salvation;
for you I wait all day long.

John 16:12-13

¹²I still have many things to say to you,
but you cannot bear them now.
¹³When the Spirit of truth comes,
he will guide you into all the truth;
for he will not speak on his own,
but will speak whatever he hears,
and he will declare to you
the things that are to come.

Mark 4:35-40

³⁵On that day, when evening had come,
he said to them,'Let us go across to the other side.'
³⁶And leaving the crowd behind,
they took him with them in the boat, just as he was.
Other boats were with him.
³⁷A great windstorm arose,
and the waves beat into the boat,
so that the boat was already being swamped.
³⁸But he was in the stern, asleep on the cushion;
and they woke him up and said to him
'Teacher, do you not care that we are perishing?'
³⁹He woke up and rebuked the wind,
and said to the sea,'Peace! Be still!'
Then the wind ceased, and there was a dead calm.
⁴⁰He said to them,'Why are you afraid?
Have you still no faith?'

— Who is my God? —

Searching for the presence of God

Romans 1:19-20

19For what can be known
about God is plain to them,
because God has shown it to them.
20Ever since the creation of the world
his eternal power and divine nature,
invisible though they are,
have been understood
and seen through the things he has made.

Who is Jesus? Who is the Father?

John 14:6-9

6Jesus said to him,
'I am the way, and the truth, and the life.
No one comes to the Father except through me.
7If you know me,
you will know my Father also.
From now on you do know him
and have seen him.'
8Philip said to him,
'Lord, show us the Father,
and we will be satisfied.'
9Jesus said to him,
'Have I been with you all this time, Philip,
and you still do not know me?
Whoever has seen me has seen the Father.
How can you say, "Show us the Father"?'

What is faith?

Hebrews 11:1-3, 6

1Now faith
is the assurance of things hoped for,
the conviction of things not seen.
2Indeed, by faith our ancestors received approval.
3By faith we understand that the worlds
were prepared by the word of God,

so that what is seen
was made from things that are not visible.
⁶And without faith
it is impossible to please God,
for whoever would approach him
must believe that he exists
and that he rewards those who seek him.

Deuteronomy 1:30-33   *When I was*
³⁰The Lord your God,   *carried …*
who goes before you,
is the one who will fight for you,
just as he did for you in Egypt
before your very eyes,
³¹and in the wilderness,
where you saw
how the Lord your God carried you,
just as one carries a child,
all the way that you travelled
until you reached this place.
³²But in spite of this,
you have no trust in the Lord your God,
³³who goes before you on the way
to seek out a place for you to camp,
in fire by night, and in the cloud by day,
to show you the route you should take.'

John 14:16-20   *When the*
¹⁶And I will ask the Father,   *words*
and he will give you another Advocate,   *won't come*
to be with you forever.
¹⁷This is the Spirit of truth,
whom the world cannot receive,
because it neither sees him nor knows him.
You know him, because he abides with you,
and he will be in you.

¹⁸I will not leave you orphaned;
I am coming to you.
¹⁹In a little while the world will no longer see me,
but you will see me; because I live, you also will live.
²⁰On that day you will know that I am in my Father,
and you in me, and I in you.

Facts
speaking for
themselves

John 9:30-33
³⁰The man answered,
'Here is an astonishing thing!
You do not know where he comes from,
and yet he opened my eyes.
³¹We know that God does not listen to sinners,
but he does listen to one
who worships him and obeys his will.
³²Never since the world began
has it been heard that anyone
opened the eyes of a person born blind.
³³If this man were not from God,
he could do nothing.'

'Who do
you say
that I am?'

Luke 9:18-20
¹⁸Once when Jesus was praying alone,
with only the disciples near him,
he asked them,
'Who do the crowds say that I am?'
¹⁹They answered,'John the Baptist;
but others, Elijah; and still others,
that one of the ancient prophets has arisen.'
²⁰He said to them,'But who do you say that I am?'
Peter answered,'The Messiah of God.'

— *Wisdom and Wonder* —

Isaiah 45:3   *Comfortable*
3I will give you   *with*
the treasures of darkness   *paradox*
and riches hidden in secret places,
so that you may know
that it is I the Lord,
the God of Israel,
who call you by your name.

Wisdom of Solomon 6:12-15ff   *Recognising*
12Wisdom is radiant and unfading   *wisdom*
and she is easily discerned
by those who love her
and is found by those who seek her.
13She hastens to make herself known
to those who desire her.
14 One who rises early
to seek her will have no difficulty
for she will be found sitting at the gate.
15To fix one's thought on her
is perfect understanding

Wisdom of Solomon 7:26ff   *Treasuring*
Therefore I prayed and understanding   *interiority*
was given to me. I called on God
and the Spirit of wisdom came to me.

Proverbs 8:29b-31   *The time of*
When he marked out   *the joyful*
the foundations of the earth,   *wise-child*
there I was beside him, like a little child
and I was daily his delight,
rejoicing before him always
rejoicing in his inhabited world ...

Coming *down to* *essentials*	*1Corinthians 13:1-2, 4ff* [1]If I speak in the tongues of mortals and of angels but do not have love I am a noisy gong and a clanging cymbal [2]And if I have prophetic powers, and understand all mysteries and all knowledge and if I have all faith so as to remove mountains, but I do not have love, I am nothing.
Moment by *moment*	*1 Samuel 3:4ff* 'Go, lie down; and if he calls you, you shall say, "Speak Lord, for your servant is listening".'
Contemp- *lative* *attitude*	*Ecclesiasticus (Sirach) 14:20ff* [20]Happy is the person who meditates on wisdom and reasons intelligently and reflects ... on her ways and ponders her secrets
Choosing *life*	*Deuteronomy 30:19-20* [29]I call heaven and earth to witness ... that I have set before you life and death, ...Choose life so that you and your descendents may live, [20]loving the Lord your God, obeying him and holding fast to him; for that means life to you and length of days ...

Ruth 1:16-17ff   *As later life*
[16]Do not press me to leave you   *unfolds*
or to turn back from following you!
Where you go,I will go
Where you lodge, I will lodge;
your people shall me my people,
and your God my God.
[17]Where you die, I will die-
there will I be buried.
My the Lord do thus and so to me,
and more as well, if even death parts me from you.

Deuteronomy 30:12-14   *Coming*
Obeying these commandments is not   *home*
something beyond your strength and reach;
for these laws are not in the far heavens,
so distant that you can't hear or obey them
and with no-one to bring them down to you;
nor are they beyond the ocean,
so far that no-one
can bring you their message;
but they re very close at hand
– in your hearts and on your lips –
so that you can obey them.[3]

---

21. *The Living Bible* (Coverdale House UK for Tyndale House Publ, Illinois, USA)

Knowing   *Proverbs 8:22-25*
the wonder
and the   22The Lord created me
mystery   at the beginning of his work,
    the first of his acts of long ago.
    23Ages ago I was set up, at the first
    before the beginning of the earth.
    24When there were no depths
    I was brought forth,
    when there were no springs
    abounding with water.
    25Before the mountains had been shaped,
    before the hills, I was brought forth –
    26when he had not yet made earth and fields,
    or the world's first bits of soil.
    27When he established the heavens I was there,
    when he drew a circle on the face of the deep

Asking   *John 1:37-39ff*
the right
question   37Then John's two disciples
    turned and followed Jesus.
    38Jesus looked around
    and saw them following.
    'What do you want?' he asked them.
    'Sir,' they replied, 'where do you live?'
    'Come and see,' he said.
    39So they went with him
    to the place where he was staying
    and were with him
    from about four o'clock that afternoon
    until evening.22

---

22. *The Living Bible*, ibid.

Alphabetical list by scriptural subject

---

* The designation of words in this list is based on popular 'everyday' recognition of a scripture text. Therefore the given topic or key word may appear further down the text, hence the ff indicated throughout.

List of texts in biblical order

Index of Marginalia

Appendix

An Croí Centre for Personal and Scriptural Enrichment,
Baltrasna, Ashbourne, Co Meath.
Higher Diploma in Spiritual Guidance. 01 8352156 www.ancroi.ie

Grace Dieu Retreat Centre, Tramore Rd, Waterford.
Spiritual Accompaniment Course. 051 374417
http://homepage.eircom.net/~gracedieu

Manresa House Jesuit Centre for Spirituality,
Diploma Course in Spiritual Direction
426 Clontarf Rd. Dublin 3
01 8331352 www.jesuit.ie/manresa

AISGA
All Ireland Spiritual Guidance Association
c/o Milltown Park, Sandford Rd, Dublin 6. www.aisga.org

Presence – The Journal of Spiritual Directors International
http://www.sdiworld.org